rebel therapy

a therapist journey through addiction, trauma, and Nichiren Buddhism

Some names and identifying details have been changed to protect the privacy of individuals. I have tried to recreate events, locales, and conversations from my memories of them. In order to maintain their anonymity, in some instances I have changed the names of individuals and places, I may have changed some identifying characteristics and details such as physical properties, occupations and places of residence.

Although I have made every effort to ensure that the information in this book was correct at time of publishing, I do not assume and hereby disclaim any liability to any party for any loss, damage, or disruption caused by errors or omissions, whether such errors or omissions result from negligence, accident, or any other cause.

This book is not intended as a substitute for the medical advice of physicians. The reader should regularly consult a physician on matters relating to his/her health and particularly with respect to any symptoms that may require diagnosis or medical attention.

This book as my views and beliefs are not endorsed nor sanctioned by the SGI. Any further information, please contact the author.

Table of Contents

matilde tomat

Matilde Tomat MBACP is a counsellor, therapist, recovery coach, specialist mentor, chaplain, writer; and a Perfect Daughter.

Born in Italy at the end of the 60's, she studied and travelled extensively until she settled in Lancashire. She has been a teacher, a tutor, a coach, a mentor; and also, a popcorn popper and a sunflower pollinator when not writing or photographing. Since arriving in the UK, she studied Counselling & Psychotherapy and realised she could not run away from the addiction that was always present in her family: she embraced her past and founded **The Resting Tree**; to inspire and support people in recovery from addiction, and their families; to get them engaged and focused; to infuse hope, to help them discover various options and possibilities, to assist them in creating their own future, to support them in envisioning a reachable goal; to discover and follow their Call to Mission. Since then, she has created an effective (and intense) 6-week programme in a residential rehabilitation center, and a series of successful workshops which include her knowledge of Counselling, Teaching, Spirituality and Philosophy, Creative Writing, and Self-Development.

Her e-book *"The Men at my White Table"* can be found on Amazon.co.uk

A practicing Nichiren Buddhist, a strong believer in Erikson's theory of development, and a fighter for the respect of human rights and the dignity of all people, she is presenting now a brand-new series of workshops.

For any further information regarding sessions, group therapy, coaching and mentoring, the 6-week recovery programme, workshops and talks, handouts and the booklet on recovery *Changing Habits Together*, please contact the author directly.

You can follow her on
fb: https://www.facebook.com/therestingtreelancs/
Twitter : @therestingtree

The music she listened to while writing this book can be found on Spotify > Playlists > my writing vibe

Acknowledgments

I would not have been here if it weren't for: Piero Tomat, Davide Marciano, dott. Paolo Eppinger, Fabio Grimaz, dott. Lezzi, Cesare Nonino, Nicoletta Bello, Giovanni Villa, Margherita e Roberto Maniacco, Kari Edwards, Sam Crapnell, Luc Jannes, Kerry Gormley.

This book would not have been written if it weren't for: David Kemp, Fran Cullen, Helen Boswell, Edel McGinn, Bob Buckley, Niki Agliolo; and all my clients and students.

I would like to personally thank the people in my private and imaginary Board of Directors:

The Therapists: Stephen Grosz, Irvin Yalom, Emmy van Deurzen

The Writers: Stephen King, Elizabeth Gilbert, Patti Smith

The Stimuli: Tony Robbins, Gary Vaynerchuk, Alain de Botton

The Gurus: James Redfield, Deepak Choprah, Wayne Dyer

The Sisters: Diane Keaton, Audrey Hepburn, Rita Levi Montalcini

MATILDE TOMAT

Dedicato a mamma e papà
e Giancarlo Lezzi

… and Marianne, Adam, Richard, Paul
all the ones we have lost along the way.

It is not so easy writing about nothing.
[Patti Smith - M Train]

This is only a note
To say how sorry I am
You died. You will realize
What a position it puts
Me in. I couldn't really
Have died for you if so
I were inclined.

[W. S. Graham - Dear Bryan Wynter]

preface

It was the 15th of August 1988. It was a sunny day.

I was 20 and I didn't know that my life would have changed at 10.30 am.

Forever.

The last thing I remember was the feeling of coldness and static of the white plastic chair by the pool, on the back of my thighs when I was about to sit. I could feel my hair, there, almost pulled. I don't remember sitting.

I have been told that I started screaming, jumped and then lost conscience.

I don't remember anything else. The doctors in A&E dismissed the whole thing simply as: "it was an extremely hot day and she had a panic attack. A massive panic attack, but nothing more".

The only thing I know is that I shut down. The following days, weeks, months are all in a blur. I remember only wanting to eat lemons, needing to be covered in wool, that I sat anywhere my parents put me, and rocked back and forth, back and forth. I felt lonely, desperate. Whatever my thoughts were, I could not express them; I was forgetting everything and did not remember the basics of living: I could not recognise any sensation, emotions, feeling. Nothing. I was zeroed. Resat beyond my control. It took me about one year to consciously leave the comfort of my bedroom, 8 years to trust someone to drive me around, 15 years to get a driving licence, 21 years to sleep alone, in a house, by myself.

I could only assume, at that time, that I was losing the plot. My thoughts made no sense, and when my emotions started to come back, they were extremely intense, and I could not differentiate, for example, between feeling hysterical or just being moved by something. Everything was desperation, disaster, pain, hurt; I felt closer to death than alive. I wished Death would come but I was way too scared to call her in.

I definitely felt not understood. And nothing made sense.

That day, that 15th August 1988, wasn't the first time I lost something precious and felt excruciating pain. It definitely wasn't the last time. But on that day, I learned the most important lesson I could have ever learned; the lesson that, at the age of 44, made me decide to throw everything I thought I knew to the wind and to go back to the roots: back to school, back to me, and made me become a counsellor. Then, a chaplain.

The lesson was: there is a part of me, a tiny tiny minimal infinitesimal minuscule part of me that is still ok. I am going to be ok, I am going to go back to be that 20-year-old woman who travelled the world alone, who was strong and happy. I haven't lost everything. There's this tiny tiny minimal infinitesimal minuscule part of me which will get larger and deeper and stronger, and everything is going to be ok. I can build on that spec of me. And I love Life.

Little did I know that it was that 20-year-old woman, who was allegedly strong and happy, the one who led me to lose everything.

I believe that I experienced Hope, then.

Every time I speak to a client I remember that same kind of pain, and desire to feel better; their belief that they are ok, that it is going to be ok, no matter what. That's there is nothing *really* wrong with them. Every time I say goodbye to a client, I try to imagine their sense of Hope, because now they are ready to go on without the support of therapy. I am then ready to wave them good-bye.

Every time a friend calls because they want to talk, or someone reads a horoscope or has tarot cards read, or they receive the first text message from someone they fancy, or a stranger smiles at them: it all goes back to Hope. Please, tell me it is going to be ok.

Hope.

> *Please, tell me it is going to be ok,*
> *that I haven't suffered all this pain for anything,*
> *that my time will come,*
> *that this is a Life worth living.*

My life has been neither better nor worse than anybody else's. I suffered, I laughed, I played, I studied, I cried, I moved; I lost people along the way and new people came in into my life; some days I cried out of total desperation, others I could not care less. I experienced both physical and emotional pain, I felt both loved and abandoned; I craved both affections and to be left alone. I survived a natural disaster, I underwent a difficult surgery, and I experienced an emergency landing in a 747, movie-style. I felt scared, I have visited war zones, I am moved by kids in tears, and I am angry at mothers burying their faces in mobile phones. Ignorance and narrowmindedness take me to the edge of anger; I do feel exasperation. At times I wanted to be a mother and now I miss the experience because it is too late.

I can feel peaceful and can be fucking fuming; I pray and dance, and I still study, every day of my life.

I crave for life, and I have learned to love the unknown and adventure.

I am scared but I try not to be anxious; injustice and hurt animals are the two most prominent subjects that make me cry. I am moved by Beauty, always.

Still, I am not a vegetarian, I don't run, I don't do yoga and I am very bad at recycling.

And I can be righteously judgemental.

Hello, I am a human being.

The story of this book is long and winded. It started somehow in July 2016. No, what am I saying! Well before that.

Somehow the story of this book is part of the book itself, and everything will become hopefully clear in the last pages. Every single event in my life and every single word written in here, is a prelude to the book itself. This book is my story and it is from the heart; but (if you are a therapist or someone more interested in some psychotherapeutic and spiritual approaches) you will also find some theory, especially in the chapter #rebeltherapy. I am aware that I should probably have someone proof-reading it, and double-checking my

English grammar, the consistency of tenses and if the whole structure makes sense. I know of other books, though, which have been highly criticised for their syntax and composition, and still be enjoyable, readable, and inspirational. One for all: *The Celestine Prophecy*. I am more interested in you getting my heart, and not that subjects, verbs, and objects are in the correct order.

Please, rest assured that I put every possible care in the writing of this book, together with the awareness that I cannot (nor want to) control your judgement.

MATILDE TOMAT

I am that.

You are that.

All this is that.

That's all there is.

[Vedic Saying]

0.000000000000000000000000000001%

Start with what you have.

I don't remember when I discovered that I wasn't totally crazy. I don't know if the first thought was: *I have lost it all.* Followed by: *if you can think that, you haven't lost it all.*

I remember walking around, looking at people and things, touching objects as for the first time, and the last time, all at the same time. Time was actually pretty gone for me. And I was experiencing the futility of it all.

I felt that the *me* of the past, the One-that-was, was gone. Completely; which to me meant feeling that I was locked in a cage. It was a golden cage, don't get me wrong, but it was still a cage. On top of this, I lost most of my memories and the ability to feel sensations in my body and to recognise them for what they really were. I could go for days without peeing. I just didn't feel the need (I was also barely drinking and eating), I didn't recognise that sensation; I don't know if there was no sensation, or the urge was there, but I didn't feel it or recognise it. I remember then being very weak once my bladder was emptied, and experiencing shivers, cold sweats, and trembling muscles. This made me feel very scared and I dreaded going to the loo for months.

I can say now that it felt like if the whole Matilde-system was being reset thanks to a virus. Everything scared me: lights on, lights off: I could not make up my mind. I simply felt, most of the time, that my life was finished, and that I had been catapulted into different time and space and everything was new, and no one understood my state of frightened wonder. Whoever Matilde had been, that wonderful easy-going, on and off planes, travelling alone, speaking different languages, amazing dancer, bright mind, perfect globetrotter, who loved and felt loved and could resolve a system of equations with her eyes closed, was gone. She did not exist anymore.

I was spending most of my time in a house where tension was so palpable it was enveloping you, and so suffocating you could not breathe. It had its own texture and consistency. I was in a house with two alcoholic parents, a younger sister, and no support but for an immeasurable amount of judgement and fear coming from the rest of the extended family: more of alienation which I experienced as blame. It was the end of the 80's and my (at the time) family reputation did not allow for any AA or anything similar, because we were *different*, we were *better*, and *no one* could understand us.

I was left with one session of group therapy where I went back home somatising everybody else's sensations and fears (think about *Three Men On A Boat!*): for the following week I was sure I suffered from everything: hallucinations, psychosis, a stroke, and a unique fear of ham (!).

I was left with one single session with a psychiatrist. Only one because my mother told me that *those people* wanted to change me, and she didn't like it, because she knew best what was good for me. Two things I remember from that single session: him explaining to me that he could understand my approach to life just by observing how I was holding a cup of coffee; and that when I asked him if he thought I was at risk of suicide, he simply replied: "*Yes. Shall I see you next week?*"

I went back to University. Prof. Bacigalupo was explaining Hamlet while I locked myself into a cubicle thinking: "*I may as well do it now if I have to do it. Why waiting?*" and just stayed there. I don't think I thought about anything. My mind probably went blank, again. My heart was racing, as usual. My head felt like exploding, as usual. I feared everything, including dying. What a coward! Disappointing everyone, including myself. Pusillanimous, my mother used to call me. She loved Latin. She was right.

In the end, I stood up and left.

I realised at that moment that I could think. I could make up a series of thoughts which had their own sense of logic. And my kind of logic screamed "preservation". That has been the *leitmotif* of most of my life: I almost died twice even before I was born, and still, I was there. I survived a natural disaster, and I was still there. I survived surgery, a motorbike accident: I was still there.

My "wanting to be here" has never been a conscious decision, but the sum of millions of little acts I seem to be doing every day.

When I work with clients who are suicidal, I always ask them if they want to die-die, I mean: really die, or if they want to die "just for today": because it is today that is unbearable; today and some of the yesterdays that remind us of that pain. It is never tomorrow. Our brain, some say, cannot compute death, so much so that *thanatophobia* (or fear of death) does not actually exist: how can you be scared of something that you don't know and haven't experienced? You can fear loneliness, abandonment, cold, darkness; and for some, death is all of the above together. Still, we don't know. We don't really know because No One has ever come back to prove to us all what's on the other side so that we would all agree.

That afternoon, I chose life. I chose to believe that there was that part of me, that tiny 0.00000000000000000000000000 0001% that I could still recognise as *Me*, Matilde. That is the only thing I knew, that is the only thing I had, and the only thing I could bring to the table. I could think. My body might have completely given up on me and at times my mind had a life of her own that I was not participating in, but that *Me* was there. Sometimes hidden, sometimes shouting, sometimes singing a lullaby, or whispering "I love you" every night I went to bed. *Me* was keeping my desires alive.

My life ended on August the 15th, 1988.

My Life began on that 15th August 1988.

When you can't tell
your friends
from your enemies,
It's time to go.
[M – Quantum of Solace]

MATILDE TOMAT

#rebeltherapy

Start with Me and You, in the Maze of Theory.

Because I just feel the need to pacify someone.

"I want to change, but not if it means changing". This sentence somewhat summarizes Stephen Grosz's book *The Examined Life* and at the same time the 'challenge' that every therapist faces with his client, regardless of the model they are using.

I define myself as an eclectic therapist, a bit of Pippy Longstocking, a rascal, a maverick, something a bit different. I have always seen myself as a sort of a dissident, heretic, heterodox, definitely non-conformist, and very unorthodox; a misbeliever at times, a fiery protester, definitely unusual, unconventional, schismatic, the odd-one-out, the irregular, the anomalous, atypical, and unrepresented at best of times. Different.

Do you recognise yourself in these definitions? Do you also feel that you don't fit? That there's not a large enough job/life description for you?

Well, let me ask you one thing: who wants to be like everybody else? Who wants to disappear among the masses? When I was about 11 I cried for my first pair of jeans. I remember that probably Benetton at the time came out with some fancy coloured ones. I cried because I wanted a pair and I wanted to be different. Little did I know, that we all cried, and we all got the jeans, and we all looked the same. Vanishing in the denim sea. Disappearing. Thinking back, I can't help but be reminded of *The Wall*, by Pink Floyd. Sadly, if I look around me now, I can't help but be reminded of the same. Go outside and look at people: all the same, wearing similar clothes, same haircut, watching the same programs, listening to the same music, doing the same things, going on holiday to the same places year in, year out; having the same arguments, repeating the same mistakes, and voting for the same people. Brain washed, holding on to a pale idea of identity because someone chooses Android over Mac. Whoopee!

If you feel different, and that no one understands you, and that you find it difficult for you to fit in, please remember that this also means that you are unique, exceptional, extraordinary, creative, fantastic, eccentric, definitely original, funny, bizarre, rare, exotic, mysterious, remarkable, wonderful and maybe a bit naughty.

You are an indisputable member of my tribe.

***

"I don't consider myself a counsellor or a therapist; I see myself more of a facilitator, a catalyst of change. My approach is definitely eclectic."

I remember when I said these words the first time, to my supervisor. I repeat them now aloud: and it still is freeing, and less arrogant. The first time I was trembling and not so sure I would be taken seriously. Now, after over 450 hours of 1-to-1's, over 500 hours of group therapy, and almost 200 hours of mentoring and together with the experience of my rehab work and workshops, I know that this is the best definition by far: it is what suits me, it describes how I work; and defines who I am. Because there is no difference between the *me* being *me*, and the *me* being "*a therapist*". I was trained in Person Centred (purely Rogerian) for the first two years of my studies, which I do strongly believe is the basis of any valid [therapeutic] relationship. At the same time, I believe that therapy needs to put an emphasis on the whole person (body, feeling, emotions, intellect, soul, spirit, and expressivity) and, hence, my role is to be there with the clients to facilitate their self-actualization (Maslow) and for them to develop into fully-functioning people (Rogers). There is a quote from a movie I watched which somehow summarises the basic concept behind any session:

You're an emotional jigsaw,
you need to piece yourself back together.
Start with the corners;
and look for the blue bits.[1]

And as a facilitator, you "just stay there" looking at them putting their pieces back together.

In my session, I use different approaches and skills: PC, Gestalt, TA. I always suggest trying new forms of expressions (writing, scrapbooking, catharsis exercises and possibly behaviouristic phenomenology); I try to tune in and mirror body language, verbal language, and behaviour during the sessions and pay attention and reflect back to changes in body language and attitude; I might also mirror and exaggerate feelings, emotions, and behaviours. I do differ

---

[1] Man Up (2015) with Simon Pegg and Lake Bell

somehow from the Humanistic view in certain instances since I do believe in taking theory into the room if appropriate: I strongly believe in treating clients as equal and showing them intellectual respect.

I am not scared of bringing spirituality into the sessions if issues of trust, hope, and faith in the future might show an indication that exploring beliefs could be of help. Griffith states that therapists tend to be dissuaded from discussing spirituality by "concerns about imposing their belief systems on their clients, convictions that reliance on God was disempowering of people, and a fear that religious differences between client and therapist could put a barrier between them". Should I have to define my approach with just one word, as a practising Nichiren Buddhist, I would use the word *Kyo* (literally vibration, voice, sutra) but which encompasses the Oneness of the Mind (Therapy), Oneness of the Body (Action) and Oneness of the Environment (Relations, starting for the one-to-one relationship between therapist and client, which is assessed and explored as a possible mirror of external relationships and needs). The word *Kyo* also includes both the latent and manifested expressions of the Self, which are the basis of therapy.

I find fascinating how counselling theory, philosophy, and Buddhism merge and fuse themselves into each other. Whether I consider the word *Kyo* as above, or the Three Truths of *ke, ku,* and *chu*[2], I notice how along the way during these past 5 years I changed, developed, and attuned myself to a path which unfolded itself in front

---

[2] For any further in-depth explanation, please see R. Causton (1995)

of me. As someone fascinated by the 'big question' of existentialism, also as a chaplain, I can only explain how I perceive the theory of thought and the healing process comparing them to a sheet of paper: a whole sheet which cannot exist without Side A and Side B. All three are inseparable from each other. The same is for my own Self, me as Matilde: my temporary Body (*ketai*, or simply *ke*) cannot exist without my eternal spiritual aspect, or Soul (*kutai*) while the Middle Way, the Mind (*chutai*) tries to make sense of it all[3] (Causton). Everything correlates and shows continuity. Distress and disease happen when the three aspects are not consistent anymore.

This is how I see and approach the clients: the ones with eating disorders who did not accept their *ke* or try so hard to become and look like someone else; Cx who told me that he had lost his *ku* along the way; Cy, whose *chu* rationalises everything but the pain of her *ku* is still so unbearable that she needs to mortify *ke*; hence, she self-harms. Not to mention my experience with people in recovery from addiction: they are the ones who ask the 'big questions', who firmly believe that Life is painful, and this pain of living is unbearable, because one day it will simply be all over; Life will end, and the whole process of living (if living is suffering) makes no sense. Death in Buddhism, instead, is seen as necessary in order to understand Life. One cannot exist without the

---

[3] I noticed how my *ke* experiences time and hence "fear of death", my *ku* suggests I am eternal, and my *chu* freaks out trying to make sense of both. Am I going to live forever, or am I going to die? How do I know?

other, as much as Good can only exist and be understood because of Evil.

At the same time, this approach helps me to recognise the difference between clients; and with me. If I saw two clients with the same *ke* (external appearance), their *ku* and *chu* would be different; or if I met a client who had a past history similar to mine and hence the reasoning and reactions might also be analogous to mine (so much that you could perceive a sense of affinity in the room) our *ku* would still be definitely unique. It is this *recognition of uniqueness* that I believe allows any client to learn to trust the process and open up with the therapist.

My own journey from the beginning of my practice (unknown even to myself at times) has meant aligning my Three Truths: the passing of time of *ke*, which fed my *chu* with knowledge and understanding to allow my *ku* to bloom and resonate with the environment. What I do now is refining my mission, and this is something I could not have done ten or twenty years ago: at that time, I did not even know my Mission. I hated anything connected with addiction and recovery. It seems, looking back, that I kept my resolve of being simply happy, no matter the obstacles, the pain, the laziness, temptations, hang-ups, and adversities. "Success typically comes only to those who persist" teaches Lickerman. And then, once I accepted my adversities, made peace with them, and learned from them, I initially found my Mission in creating value for other people. I learned that life can be treacherous and painful. Still, it is worth the effort, because I have chosen to see endless promises, potentials, and possibilities. This is the end of apathy (van Deurzen, 2015). A shift into all this has happened when I decided consciously not to be a victim anymore and, instead, accept responsibilities (Rowan, 1998); and to create and express myself using art in various forms. This allowed me not to compare myself anymore with people whom I identified with while trying frustratingly to reproduce their road to success (believing underneath that it would not work for me *anyway*) but to cherish my own uniqueness. When I stopped rescuing people, then I learned to apply self-care. Comparison at that point became a possible drive and not an irritating and discouraging obstruction. I learned to believe in my talents and to trust myself, I became more optimistic without overestimating my own abilities. While in the past I simply thought I was someone definitely better than others, this process helped me turn into someone better; in this case, someone better than I previously was. I had to change, and I accepted change. I constantly remind myself to embrace change even now; to drop any resistance to change; to be open to change. This journey of growth and change began when I was born, and it will end in this body when I die. It is a continuum. Consciously, it began while reading *The Celestine Prophecy* in 1996. From that moment, I read, tried, tested, asked, studied various theories, approaches, spiritualties, the healing process and holistic therapies. *None worked, all worked.* This is why I believe in eclecticism, which is nothing else than bringing onto the table a varied menu depending on the degree of hunger, the desires, the needs, the seasons and festivities, who is invited, and the ingredients available.

Eclecticism is "the practice of choosing doctrines from various or divers systems of thought in the formation of a body of acceptable doctrine (…) it does not doubt all systems (…) it does not modify all (…) rather it selects from each its psychologically satisfying doctrines." (Woolfe). I also like the notion that it is very real, technical, empirical and somehow atheoretical. Of course, eclectics can at times be seen as charlatans and as showing a lack of determination, centeredness, and sophistication. Others argue that instead, eclectics are more open to the needs of the clients without being purists and pedantic (Woolfe). I could argue that first and foremost, before any labelling, and sitting in front of the clients, it is me. And my integrity. And my congruence. I also find somehow sad when eclectics are considered intellectually lazy, with no rigour nor discipline, as people who play it by ear. 'In Britain, it tends to evoke an unremitting negative connotation which makes practitioners avoid using the term – even if it may be best descriptive of their practice. (Woolfe). Eclecticism, for it to work, must still have a structure and be systematic, coherent to be effective since it is not simply borrowing and stitching together various methodologies. Not to mention that not pledging allegiance to any particular school nor therapeutic dogma provides a sense of freedom (Egan). To cut the long story short, eclecticism is not chaos.

In my work with clients, as in my personal journey of discovery, I have noticed the need for meaning and purpose, and to make sense of the Why behind Life; I have observed the fear of making choices and how frightening freedom can be; how difficult it is to start taking responsibilities; how necessary it is to learn from experience, and how learning is always connected to relationships. This is existentialism in a nutshell: the approach that strives to see clients as 'flesh and bone' and not just 'mind'; as freely choosing beings, as subjects, as an undividable whole. In order to see the client as a whole, the therapist needs to bring his/her wholeness to the relationship 'right down to their wordless depth' and being real and authentic ['*How can one have a genuine encounter with another person while remaining so opaque.* (Irvin Yalom as found in Cooper)] Some now could argue that eclecticism comes from a well-defined cauldron of humanistic practices, while my approach which also includes spirituality and existentialism/philosophy should be considered as 'pluralistic' (Cooper). I personally think we already have too many labels.

More important than asking the best way to name the approach, would be to enquire if it works. There are not many types of research available at this time which focus only on eclecticism, but mainly in comparison with other approaches, and depending on the type of treatment offers and areas of dis-ease of the clients (mainly depression and anxiety). Researches do indicate that there are small differences in the effectiveness of therapies. (Woolfe) but then again, the variables within the researches are so wide that I personally find very difficult to take as granted any research in the field. One major question that also needs to be taken into consideration regards the locus of integration and/or eclecticism: is it external (just based on the client), internal (within the therapist) or in the relationship? Not to mention that contained within the three different loci of integrations, there are present sub-groups and definitions. Research in counselling is complicated since there is a theoretical difficulty in replicating the data collection since the whole point of therapy is adaptability, change and fluidity and all is very subjective.

I can only think with respect to my own clients, and one in particular. Cy lives in a sense of constant alienation and fear:

'I was much further out than you thought
and not waiving, but drowning..."

[van Deurzen]

Any type of purist therapy previously tried did not work (in Cy's own words) and I could (and still can) only base my therapeutic rapport with her on the suggestion of Irvin Yalow: "It is the relationship that heals" (Cooper). After having assessed with my supervisor and the agency rep. that I was working within the service level framework as described by the CPCAB and that I was comfortable and safe in working with her; and that she would have been safe with me, I could only work in a therapeutic setting on a session-by-session basis. Isn't this anyway the approach that any therapist uses, albeit unconsciously?

What M. Barkham (in Dryden) has found is that it seems that up to now research has been mainly focused on the figure of the therapist rather than on the actual validity of the techniques and that most of the times, when a therapist feels threatened by the client, his (or her) strategy is to revert to specific therapeutic techniques. I have personally found, instead, that defining myself as eclectic, allows me also to dive fully into any approach should I find myself expected in doing so but still within the skills and knowledge of said approach. Even if in a totally different setting, my role as a chaplain allows me to use my listening and counselling skills within a purist person-centred approach, where my role and the expectations of the end-users are of a temporal (mostly one-off) and (mostly silent) spiritual support.

What I personally find attractive and productive, as in the words of Arthur Schnitzler (Frankl), is funding my approach on objectivity (with the assistance of my supervisor), courage and responsibility; hoping (and waiting) for a research methodology which really and thoroughly addresses eclecticism.

Because in my personal journey I found that different things worked for me at different times, I use the same type of approach with my clients.

And I am wondering: what about you? Do you prefer a body of knowledge that sits within a well-defined, tried and tested approach and sticks to it, no matter what? Do you like the comfort of a category? Its labelling? Because there's nothing wrong with that, too. Especially, if it works for you. And then, we are both happy.

But if by any chance you feel that you might *need* something else, something *different*, that whatever you are trying is not working for you as you expected, because no matter what, there is still this feeling of not being content, not feeling settled, like if something is still missing: please, I want you to know that changing, testing, trying, and not feeling content is ok, too.

With the exception of extremes and abuse, there is no right or wrong in therapy. You can choose whatever is best for you, and then you can change your mind again, and go back to what you swore you will never try just because you have changed. And it's ok.

Don't get me wrong: you will find students, out there, and therapist who swear by their well-defined approach as being absolutely *The Best*, ever! I am happy for them, for having found something so definite. I am also happy for their clients if they find what they are looking for.

I remember Stephen King[4] describing some writing workshops as full of people "nodding, smiling, and looking solemnly thoughtful". God only knows I have taken part in workshops, meetings, and trainings among people who have been "nodding, smiling, and looking solemnly thoughtful" where my soul was screaming and my body itching because I felt no real participation, no awareness, no passion, no drive; and where I also found no depth and no wisdom; where I wasn't getting anything, but the confirmation of what I needed, wanted, looked and worked for.

"I'm drowning here, and you're describing the water!"

[Melvin Udall - "As Good As It Gets"]

I only know that I am *me*, and I do not want to sell my clients something that I don't personally believe in. I know, I am a rebel. And this is why I like to call my approach #rebeltherapy.

There's something of a rebellious streak in all of us.
Usually it's dormant, but sometimes it's provoked into expression.
If nurtured and guided with wisdom and compassion, it can be a positive force
that frees us from fear and ignorance. If it manifests neurotically, however,
full of resentment, anger, and self-interest,

---

[4] "And, instead of pelting these babbling idiots with their own freshly toasted marshmallows, everyone else sitting around the fire is often nodding and smiling and looking solemnly thoughtful." - Stephen King, *On Writing: A Memoir of the Craft*

then it can turn into a destructive force that harms oneself
as much as it does others.
When confronted with a threat to our freedom or independence
and that rebellious streak surfaces,
we can choose how to react and channel that energy.
It can become part of a contemplative process that leads to insight.
Sometimes that insight comes quickly,
but it can also take years.
[Dzogchen Ponlop – Rebel Buddha]

You need to be a rebel to start a revolution, your personal revolution; you need to be a *rebelutionary* if you want to embark in what Nichiren Buddhists call "Human Revolution": the change within you.

This Revolution needs only one rebel.

It starts here.

It starts now.

It starts with you.

***

This book is my journey. Nothing more than that: the stories, the experiences, the lessons learned, and what worked for me. If you don't find anything of assistance in the book, I still hope that your journey is light and that you find the right support. Maybe your role is just to pass this book onto someone else. My hope is that you discover resilience, in these pages, if nothing else. I hope that you believe that things really do change, that everything really works out for the best, and that it is not ended until you say it is finished.

If you think that you will find "The Truth" among these pages, a brand new amazing theory and approach that will cure your life of all your problems, with codes and exercises and a step-by-step path to follow to the letter "because I know (best)" due to my shiny diplomas so well exhibited on my power wall, and you will be finally happy: I am sorry, but this is not that kind of a book. If you are hoping to find the link to the chapter on "ailments, healing, exercises, and recovery", again: this is not the type of book.[5]

If you think that you can find in these pages the (over-inflated) Personality, the Influencer, the Public Figure, the Futurist who will motivate you to *grind* and will persuade you with badly researched quotes and a couple of handfuls of theatrical common sense floating on some dramatic music, you are (hopefully) wrong again and I would suggest checking the real meaning of those descriptions once embedded in reality; and, referencing the comedian Josh Widdicombe, maybe reassessing some of your priorities, in the meantime, too.

This book is about a specific journey: my journey. And it is a journey in itself. And it is a bit of a wake-up call.

This book doesn't end. My journey doesn't end, and recovery doesn't exist: you were not wrong, damaged, nor corrupt before that you need *changing* now. You are not *clean* now, because you have never been dirty before. Moreover, if "recovery" really existed, how long do

---

[5] "There is no one *treatment of choice* for trauma, and any therapist who believes that his or her particular method is the only answer to our problems is suspect of being an ideologue rather than somebody who is interested in making sure you get well. No therapist can possibly be familiar with every effective treatment and he or she must be open to your exploring options other than the ones he or she offers. He or she must also be open to learning from you." (van der Kolk, 2014, p. 212). He couldn't have putting it better.

you want it to be? For how many days/weeks/months/years do you want to be labelled as "in recovery"? And why?

If you think that "recovery never ends", that has another name: it is called Life.

God placed
the best things
in life
on the other side
of fear.
[Will Smith]

thanks, Gary!

Start with the truth.

I have woken up one day convinced that the idea of writing this book about my journey, was a great idea, an amazing idea. It would be fantastic! Great! Smashing!

But now I am sitting here, at my laptop. I am trembling and part of me is dreading the idea of describing what my life has really been because I know that I will feel. Again.

As much as I am feeling now: tight shoulders, stiff neck, a knot in my stomach. This just to start with, and these sensations have been lingering in me for the past week when I read in my journal (and was reminded by my Google Calendar) that I should sit and write if I wanted this book to be out. A book doesn't write itself.

I mean, I could not do it. I could stop now and decide that it is not for me, at least not now. This is not the right time, for me. I could ring my two dear friends whom I discussed this idea and tell them that the deadlines we have worked out together are not applying to me anymore.

I could.

And this is one of the last lessons I have learned but decided to pass on to you first: I can *choose*. I can do anything. I do not have to explain, justify anything to anyone. And so, can you.

If you are at a cross-road in your life (and if you are reading this, you might be) please, do remember: you can *always* choose.

At times we feel compelled to decide, to choose between A and B and we think, and think again, and ask so many questions, and advice, and suggestions, and feedback to family members, friends, relatives, colleagues, professionals, therapist, books and YouTube bloggers. We do not know how to make up our mind. And this indecisiveness is painful, time-consuming; it is exhausting.

What about choosing, for the time being, *consciously* not to choose? Shall I change my job, shall I go back to college, shall I call her, shall I break up with him, shall I move, shall I…? One of the most freeing emotions, for me, was to find within me the assertiveness of making a choice, of choosing by myself. And, at times, this choice was 'not to choose': I am not ready yet.

I choose not to choose.

Of course, you already choose not to choose, without realising. We always, and I repeat *always*, choose; we are always autonomous in making up our own decisions. Sometimes we think we aren't because life has given us that kind of family, that situation, those friends, that disease, that nationality, that skin colour we cannot escape from.

Still, we can always all choose: how we see things, how we approach things, if we are leaving, moving, cutting people out for good.

Learning to own our decisions is what differentiates us from children and makes us adults, fully functioning and autonomous adults. We are, in the end, the only authority, the only Legitimate Authority in our lives.

So, following the great words of the 21st century supreme blogger Gary Vayernchuck, I say *Fuck Fear*, let's do this.

Let me feel all of these feelings because this fear, this emotional pain I am experiencing now is only a vestigial of what I felt then, and because of some reasons. Are those reasons still valid now? I am now a different person, I have grown, I can take care of myself now. It is only a matter of reminding myself of this. Every day, and some days, every hour. And it is ok.

The same applies to you, now, reader.

You can choose to read on, to follow the options provided, to like or not to like this book, to pass it on, or chuck it in the bin, to choose to try, or to choose it is not your time yet, because you don't feel that the time is right for you. And it is ok. I am ok with any of that. Are you ok?

This book is not going to tell you that you have to try any of the things I tried and that if they worked for me, they will *definitely* work for you. This book is my experience and my only hope is for you to read it and somewhere, anywhere, among these words, for you to find one sentence, one hint, one emotion, one sensation that resonates with you and that gives you, maybe, a bit of courage, a pinch of understanding, a knowledge that you are going to be ok, as much as it might feel and be hard now: you are going to be ok. In the end, everything works out for the best.

Of course, we all have to do our part. As of now, your only part could simply be choosing to get this book and keep it on the shelf. Or, get this book and read it. Or get this book and act upon it. Because, and here it comes: we need to do something. Reading without action, living without action, surviving without action is just reacting to the decisions of others.

Again, some days your action can be deciding not to do anything because everything seems very hard; another day your action could become: *I am going to wash myself and open those blinds*; one day it will turn into *I'm going out to do some shopping, for a walk, to my GP, to meet a friend, to go to the library, to look for a job, …*

The awareness that this is your choice, that is your decision, that you have made up your mind, is what makes all the difference.

> *The important thing, therefore, is to have the spirit, the determination, to improve your environment, to change it for the better, even if just a little.*[6]
> [Daisaku Ikeda]

[Please, don't give me the eye-rolling and the "*you don't know what it means…*", the "*yes, but…*", or the storming off the room. I have seen it all before and it doesn't work. Ever.]

It took me years to go from "[*nothing*]", to "*I am sick and tired of feeling like this*" to "*I'm going to eat something today*" to "*I really want a driving licence*"; from 1988 to 2004 to be honest. Some days I reverted back, some other days I jumped fast forward way too fast and way too soon, and in between, I did a lot of other things and life went on. Most of the times, though, I now recognise that I simply reacted. That does not mean that I don't do it now, but I like now to assert my own decisional ownership and say: I decide now, *consciously*, in full awareness, to sit here, and write these words, and to feel whatever it is to feel in the process.

---

[6] Ikeda, HUMAN REVOLUTION, p.51

I know that by intentionally making this decision, I am fully owning the change of direction my life might take.

And it is my decision.

When is the last time that you decided, that you fully took action, that you wilfully created your future?

When we change
the world changes.
The key to all change is our inner transformation
— a change of our hearts and minds.
This is Human Revolution.
We all have the power to change.
When we realise this truth,
we can bring forth that power anywhere,
anytime, and in any situation.

[Daisaku Ikeda]

MATILDE TOMAT

diluted nothingness

Start with the body.

I want to start with the body on purpose because I am not a doctor, nor I am qualified to give any personal suggestion. Hence, I am starting with this full disclaimer: I am not a doctor, a GP, I am not trained to assist you with the body-related part of your journey.

Still, *still…* this body-part is such an important one, in our sense of wellness, or in feeling totally out of whack. Hence, I am going to write certain things anyway.

First and foremost: let's use the proper words. You are depressed when you are diagnosed with depression. Same for being bipolar, OCD, on the *spectrum* (whatever this spectrum is), or *borderline*. Otherwise, you are very sad and moody and in transition. Do you need a label? Do you like to be labelled? Do you feel comfortable in being labelled, in suffering from a recognised disease? And then: are you depressed (i.e. do you identify with the disease) or do you suffer from depression (i.e. something that comes and then goes, and it is not *me*)? Because there is a lot of difference.

Then, if you break your leg, you need a cast. If you are feeling depressed, anxious or weak, you might need medication.

Please, go and see your GP, a doctor, a professional, one who has got all the diplomas on the wall and whom you trust: talk and discuss your wellness with them. Do not follow them blindly if you don't feel heard but look for and find another one that you feel you can trust. DO

NOT follow suggestions regarding your physical wellness if given to you by people who are not trained and who haven't got experience. Your mother, father, boyfriend or friend who tells you that you don't need to take something which has been prescribed to you by your GP, or who asks you to try what they have been given, are not your Friends, they are not Friends of your journey. And moreover, they are not you.

If you feel that you want to try something alternative, go to a serious Health Food shop, where you can be served by someone 'who knows', not simply a shop assistant, and talk to them, ask questions. Then go home and read about it. Get informed: it is your body. It is your wellness. It is your journey.

On my journey, I started with injections of Valium plus so many other medications I lost count: things to keep me calm and then stuff to raise my mood; medication for the headaches and the stomach aches I was getting because of all the other tablets I was taking; multi-minerals and multi-vitamins supplements; stuff to sleep, and other stuff to be awake; herbal drops, and more herbal drops, and herbal teas, loads of herbal teas. Basically, I was a walking chemist, on edge. Barely eating, barely sleeping. Still, I was going on and on and on. Until one day I was handed over by my father (who did not know what to do with me) to an army doctor, a very young and gorgeous doctor (wearing both his dark green combat uniform and his white scrub) who had some time on his hands and also wanted to please his superior, and who politely asked me what I was taking. Oh, gosh! I never felt so heard and proudly I opened my bag and took everything out, explaining to him bottle by bottle, blister by blister what I had with me, on me, at all times. I laid everything out, neatly. I was so happy with showing him that I was taking my illness very seriously.

He listened to me silently while looking at me at all times; then he smiled, took everything into his big manly hands, and chucked every single one into the bin.

"You don't need any of that", he told me. "You will be cured when you will find the courage to leave your family and your boyfriend". Little did I know that he was right. It took me 20 years to comprehend what he said, to me, that day. When I write "comprehend", I don't mean it intellectually: we all know what we "have to do", that the suggestions we have been given are "right" [while we think: *easy for them to say it, they are not in our shoes… tz!*]. It took me 20 years to feel and deeply live within me his words, to let them sink and make them mine; to swap his voice, with mine.

To recognise I was sick and tired of being sick and tired. For that to become my action, and not just a reaction. I have never forgotten his words, his voice, where we were sitting, how the sun was reflecting on the old windows, how many cigarettes I smoked that afternoon, how I was still burying my head and neck and shoulders in the sand. How much part of my brain, in full anxiety, did not compute any of that. Still, his words were there. Paolo Eppinger, the blue-eyed doctor, I haven't seen in years.

Let me tell you this, though: he made that drastic decision to take me off everything because he understood me, he knew my situation, he knew my physiology, he knew my reactions; he basically knew his stuff. He could do it because he was a doctor and he was the authority where medication, chemistry, and psychiatry were concerned. I trusted him; because very possibly, deep *deep* down, unconsciously, I knew he was right. Our synergy that afternoon was perfect. My wish, for you, is to find someone like my blue-eyed doctor. He then took the time to explain to me how panic attacks work, how my brain works, what I do need, what I should do. And some of these things he told me is what I am passing on to you now, including what I found along the way, that worked *for me*.

1. You need to drink water. Simple, still, lukewarm water, in small sips. The reason is that by drinking that water you are cleaning your cells, regulating your breathing (by sipping), you will be feeling refreshed (anxiety raises your temperature), and you will not provide a massive shock to your system, setting in motion the vagal nerve[7]. If during an anxiety attack you are feeling that you can't breathe in order to keep yourself calm, drink water: plain, simple, cheap, still lukewarm tap water in small sips. That will also help you restore your correct breathing pattern.

2. During phases of anxiety, panic, sadness, disconnection happens. Here's the word: *disconnection!* The body is disconnected from the mind and the soul. This is a typical symptom of people with PTSD and of

---

[7] The *Vagal* (or *Vagus* nerve) is a cranial nerve that connects the larynx, heart, lungs, and digestive tract; it also contributes to the innervation of the abdomen, viscera, and colon. Its functions are important from both a physical and an emotional spectrum. Every time we drink something too cold, or are scared by something, our heart rate increases, we start sweating and we might feel the need to defecate. That is because of our vagal nerve. When we use sentences like "it scared me to death", or "I am shitting myself", "died of fear"; or our voice disappears when anxious or in anger, it is because of this nerve (the connection of the emotional with the physical aspects of our existence).

anyone who suffered traumatic experiences. We feel that *"we are not really there"*, that life goes on without us, that we are *"out of kiln"*, or similar. Basically, our Neo Cortex (the planning system in our brain) and the Limbic System (the survival mode) do not work together. We do need to connect our body again, to make it ours, to own it and its sensations. There is plenty of research which shows how rhythm, chanting, singing, movement, and expressivity can help to heal traumatic experiences. Please, find a good friend who can hug you; or go and have a massage or acupuncture. Try singing in a choir; explore kendo, tai chi, tango. Swim, if you can. Dance: gently re-appropriating your body thanks to rhythmic movements. I remember that some of my best developmental cries have been made while swimming or under the shower. Or dancing. Sometimes we are so scared of the sensations we are feeling, that we need to shut them down completely. We freeze, and our body (our expression) freezes with us. The more we try to shut them down, the more we enter into a spiral of panic: the fear of fear. Reconnecting our body means accepting and understanding the sensations our body is feeling.

3. Quick disclosure: when I walked out of my marriage, I was 40 years old. I did not want to end up spending my weekends in discos, bar, clubbing, drinking, and possibly ending up in unhelpful short relationships. I enrolled in tango classes, instead. I didn't know anyone, nor the first thing about tango. I only remember that during the first lesson, when someone (read: a man I never met before) had to place his hands on my elbows to gently help me to simply walk following the music, something opened up in me, and I started crying. And I mean:

sobbing. I think that there must have been something so repressed, closed, frightened in me that chose that moment to come to the surface, and I let it express itself, through tears. It was probably a combination of his hands and him asking me "may I?" before touching me. Tango taught me patience, boundaries, respect, body language. I will be forever grateful for those nights spent softly swaying and rocking back and forth while waiting for someone to invite me to dance.

4. In my case, I noticed how whenever I felt I was coming back to life, I needed dance, music and to move my body following a rhythm[8]. If I could not dance for any particular reason, I walked. I know some people swear on running. I can't. I envy people who can run but running is not for me. I walk, for miles on ends. Music in my ears, and off I go. I found that walking for me is like meditation: there's a part in my brain that switches off (the worry, the anxiety, the dread, the fear) and I discover hope again. It might have to do with hormones, stress reduction, blood flow, oxygen reaching the most hidden recesses in my body and bringing them back to life, regulation of rhythm of breath, and its depth. I don't know. I am just a different person. It also helps my hunger and my digestion (thank you, vagal nerve, again). More than anything, I am allowed to daydream, make up stories with incredible happy endings, I can think straight, I can plan and organise, I revisit ideas. I connect again, I feel whole. I connect with nature, colours, animals, people and all-round Beauty. I am not alone, I am part of a

---

[8] Please, look again at *The Body Keep the Score*, by B. van der Kolk.

Whole, but I am still unique, and I don't get lost in it[9]. So, whether you prefer to run, swim, cycle, or like me walk: please, do it. Or if you prefer yoga, tai chi, chi gong: anything that moves your body. Anxiety and panic attacks are like gym exercises for the body which is so still and locked and frozen in its own emotional pain that it becomes *unsatisfied* and needs to release tension. Hence, the attacks[10]. So, move your body, dance, do sport (something that involves rhythm, since rhythm is so important!). And things will start to change.

5.   Especially at the beginning, I needed medication, and it was heavy. After that, I personally switched onto "natural and herbal" supplements. Now, I know that a lot of doctors (including personal friends) will raise their eyebrows and roll their eyes. I even used homoeopathy and sometimes I use it now, too. Many doctors, and scientists, still define it as "diluted nothingness". Whether it works simply as a placebo effect, or it really *really* works, I am not sure. I only know that it works, for me, at times. Again, I went to see a specialist and a homoeopath, had a thorough examination and followed his prescriptions[11]. Again, it might not work for you as it worked for me,

---

[9] You might want to have a look at the Walking Meditation (or mindfulness walking experience) by Thich Nhat Hanh on https://plumvillage.org/mindfulness-practice/walking-meditation/ : *Take my hand. / We will walk. / We will only walk. / We will enjoy our walk / without thinking of arriving anywhere.*

[10] This need to release tension and the body feeling unsatisfied and restless remind me of many clients (mainly men) who chose cocaine as their preferred drug, and always combine pornography with its use.

[11] *Disclaimer:* When I went to see the homeopath in Italy, back in 1999, the regulations prescribed that only a GP / doctor could become a homeopath. I am not aware of the regulations now. Please, check accordingly.

but my point here is: broaden your horizon. This is your body: if you feel that something is not working, check, read, explore, discover, ask questions, try something different. It is your journey, and whether you decide to do it by car, bicycle, or on foot, it is your decision. You cannot walk miles and miles wearing a pair of shoes which is not good for you just because someone gave it to you. Feel what your body needs. And change, if need be.

6. Food: I know that when I follow a balanced diet, I feel much better. It is not true that if you want to eat properly it is going to be more expensive. Eating a sensible diet means providing your body (including your brain/mind) with all the nutrients it needs. It does not matter to me if you are vegetarian, vegan, allergic or intolerant to something, or simply difficult. Cooking is good for you: the action of creating what you will then insert into your body, your fuel, what you feed your brain, your mood and your soul with is as important as the act of eating. Be creative, be an explorer, try different things, different foods, various associations. Have fun! If you feel that after certain foods you feel in a worse mood, bloated, heavy, and not really happy, have maybe a look at websites or books which explore Ayurveda and the Three Dosha. Ayurveda states that, depending on our body type, we "should or should not" eat certain foods, which in turn either increase or decrease our energy[12]. In my case, I noticed that even if I lived in Italy and was fed tomatoes the whole of my life, my body does

---

[12] I know it is more complicated and interesting than that, so please have a look at Deepak Chopra website on Ayurveda : https://chopra.com/articles/what-is-ayurveda and Discover Your Three Dosha as Vata Pitta Kapha : https://shop.chopra.com/dosha-quiz/ which are very good starting points.

not really agree with them. Now I avoid them when I can. I also noticed that during my pre-menopausal period, I was craving peas and flax seeds, since they do contain phytoestrogens which are hormone regulators. The point I'm trying to make here is to learn to listen to your body: do you feel hungry? What do you fancy eating? Should you believe that you are eating either too much, or too little, and you (or someone close to you) perceive this as a problem, please do seek professional help.

7. Sleep: are you sleeping enough? What do you feel when you wake up, are you still tired? For years I have been sleeping a lot and never felt refreshed. I tended to listen to audiobooks or to watch TV, and later, of course, we have all been obsessed with the phone, laptop, tablet in bed. We know that this is what creates the problem, and still, we do it. The question is: what kind of life do we want to have? What is it that I want or need to do tomorrow morning? How many hours of sleep do I need? If we are and act as, adults, we already know that in order to have a good night sleep we shouldn't have all our gadgets in the bedroom; TV and radio should be off; we should minimise noise and light. We could then, somehow, train ourselves to slip, gently, into sleep. We shouldn't also be drinking too much, eat excessively and right before going to bed. Why don't we do it then? I was watching a movie, the other day, where Kirsty Dunst says to Paul Bettany, in *Wimbledon*, "Go out there, and decide who you are". After reading these suggestions (which, don't get me wrong, are not new and are based purely on common sense) we can all decide "who we are", and what kind of people we want to be. As per the "common sense" definition: I am

mindful that many people are aware of any of the points I made before. Still, when I am at University, mentoring students, I also notice many of them very anxious and still drinking only coffees and energy drinks, while avoiding lunch altogether. It seems to me that some "common sense" hasn't reached the Student Unions.

Therefore: try. Test, explore, see what works for you. Do you want to try and change or expand your diet? What about trying to go to bed without your phone? Tomorrow maybe, try going for a walk, just to move your body and feel the effect it has on you.

Soon she will realise that she has herself
and turn to it for sustenance and comfort,
and winter will then be through[13].
[Lucy Cavendish]

---

[13] "Time to stop relying on others for that comfort, warmth, and sustenance that only true self-love can bring. Waiting for others to give you what you need will be a long and lonely, bone-chilling wait at this time. So, look at what you have, turn to it, and feast on it! Learn to love and appreciate the apple [*the Source of Hope and Light*] in your hands and save the seeds of self-love and plant them. [*From it*] comes the gift of wisdom, comes self-love, comes abundance, and comes the knowledge that you are a person who deserves to care for and love your own self. […] You will be committing to helping yourself – and then you will be free of the need of approval, shelter, and rescue. There is only one true rescue, and it comes with the miracle of self-life". (*Oracle of Shadows and Light*, by Lucy Cavedish)

If you want to understand
the causes that existed in the past,
look at the results
as they are manifested at the present.
And if you want to understand
what results will be manifested in the future,
look at the causes that exist in the present.
[Nichiren Daishonin – WND-1, 279]

follow the nib

Start from the essential.

I know that you have noticed that I have asked you some questions, along the way of these first pages. And I have also thrown there, almost un-noticeable, that quote a couple of pages back. And its footnote.

On purpose, as a footnote. Did you notice it?

Would you like to go back and read it?

Or read it again?

What do you feel?

When someone tells you that it is the time to be fully responsible, to fully take your life in your hands; that you have to stop relying on others for safety and comfort: how does it feel, for you?

Imagine being in the middle of a street, and seeing a truck, at full speed, driving right at you: what would you feel?

For a long time, until someone pointed it out at me, my automatic response would have been: "*I don't know, I move…*"

I don't know, I move.

What do you feel? *I don't know, I move.*

The question wasn't about what I would *do.*

The question is about what I would feel. *Feel.*

And that was a clear sign of my disconnection from feelings.

So, if I ask you what you feel if someone tells you that you should stop relying on others for safety and comfort, that you should start creating your life, take it into full hands and make your decisions, for your own happiness and wellbeing, what would you reply to me?

I know, I don't like the word *"should"*, too.

But this book is a bit like therapy: if you think that in here you will find solutions that magically will sort your life out, without you doing anything about it, this is the wrong book for you. If you think that in order to achieve everlasting transformation and success, you can find shortcuts without having to put in the hours, the sweat, the tears, and the pain, again: this is the wrong book. And I most certainly would be the wrong therapist for you.

I am not here to sell you an easy way out. You probably know your already (established?) outlets: drinking, smoking, too much thinking, promiscuity, too much TV, too much phone, too much work, too much escapism, anger, anxiety, blaming, gambling, pornography, too much co-dependence (I am wondering if there were ever a good amount of co-dependency). If you think that going to therapy would mean finding someone who will make the decisions on your behalf, and that, when things go wrong, you can blame, you will not grow. I really do hope there is no such a therapist out there.

I will ask those questions again: are you ready to find safety and comfort and love in yourself, and in yourself only?

Stop. Don't give me the answer now, this very moment.

Think.

What is your Inner Being saying? Nothing? What do you mean, by nothing? Can you listen to your Inner Voice? I like to call it my Inner Truth. It is like an internal GPS that nudges at me when I am on the wrong path, when I am doing things I know I shouldn't, when I am staying up too late, not eating enough, or thinking too much about something or someone. When I don't go for that walk I know it would help me. When I don't ask for help. When I don't stop and listen to me. When I am giving that answer, I know I will regret one day.

Can you listen to your voice? Can you hear it? No?

Ok, let's start with the essentials then.

Anyone who works with me knows this: my clients need to journal. Extensively.

Go out, and treat yourself to a notebook, possibly A4, a pen or pencil. Find a time a space it suits you (which means trying, and trying, and trying) and write.

And I mean, write.

Everyday.

Possibly every morning.

3 pages, every morning. It's about 750 words, I believe.

At the beginning it will take its time, your hand is going to hurt, and you will go through moments of not having any idea what to write about. Still, you sit there and write.

Write words, write *"I don't know what to write, I don't know what to write, I don't know what to write, I don't know what to write, I don't know what to write, I don't know what to write, I don't know what to write"* until your subconscious kicks in and you will be able to hear a voice saying "what's the point in all of this?" "why do I have to do this?", "I really would like to go out instead, gosh, I am already late for work, I hate writing, this exercise is stupid. Oh, my hand is hurting, and this pen is shit. Really, does this work? Wouldn't it be better to go to therapy and talk, instead? …"

Have you noticed what just happened there? Your Inner Voice is coming out. At times she will be shy, others angry, or sad. Or empty, indecisive, dreamy, funny. It will be you.

Write that.

She might show you that she is scared. Or, are you?

Write that.

The project of writing is something I have learned to do consistently and to use it therapeutically with myself, and my clients, after I did the "84 days of the Artist Way", by Julia Cameron. The experience is a 12-week course in which you are asked to write the Morning Pages, to start with.

"The bedrock tool of a creative recovery is a daily practice called Morning Pages. Morning Pages are three pages of longhand, stream of consciousness writing, done first thing in the morning. *There is no wrong way to do Morning Pages* – they are not high art. They are not even "writing." They are about anything and everything that crosses your mind– and they are for your eyes only. Morning Pages provoke,

clarify, comfort, cajole, prioritize and synchronize the day at hand. Do not over-think Morning Pages: just put three pages of anything on the page...and then do three more pages tomorrow." For any more information regarding the 84 Days of the Artist Way experience, described as a Spiritual Path to Creativity, please see Julia Cameron's pages here:

http://juliacameronlive.com/the-artists-way/

Following are some hints for you to use in your journalling for the next 12 weeks, should you decide to try, and should you feel you need some prompts instead of going full stream of consciousness You will also find more prompts at the end of this book.

Week One

1. Tell me about shame…
2. Do you believe in positive affirmations?
3. Tell me about three enemies of your self-worth…
4. Write a Thank You letter to yourself…
5. Write in your defence – and mail those pages to yourself!
6. Tell me about safety…
7. What's creativity?

Week Two

1. Who are you?
2. Who finds your creativity disturbing?
3. Who is making you crazy?
4. Tell me about attention, and what it means to you…
5. What makes you a Creative Person?
6. What do you enjoy doing, and why don't you do it?
7. List 10 tiny changes you would like to make for yourself.

Week Three

1. What are your limits?

2. Tell me about anger…

3. What's synchronicity for you?

4. What direction is your Dream?

5. Give yourself a negative and a positive feedback.

6. What does growth mean to you?

7. What's power?

Week Four

1. Selling your Integrity cheap…

2. Real feelings and Official feelings…

3. Write about things which sound like fun but that you will never do…

4. Write about silly things that you would like to try at least once…

5. Describe your ideal environment.

6. What did you do at the age of eight?

7. What's your payoff in staying stuck?

Week Five

1. How do you curtail your possibilities?

2. What's your virtue trap?

3. Tell me about your forbidden joy…

4. A wish list of 20 items: I wish… I wish… I wish… (finish the sentences)

5. what way are you mean to yourself?

6. I am blaming *xyz* for being stuck…

7. If my dream comes true, I…

Week Six

1. Tell me about abundance…

2. How are you yearning to be creative and still refusing to feed that hunger?

3. Tell me about three enemies of your self-worth…

4. In order to have money, I need to…

5. These pages you write, are a creation…

6. What's naturally abundant in your life?

7. Serious art is born from serious play!

Week Seven

1. What does listening mean to you?
2. What does connecting with others mean to you?
3. Perfectionism is…
4. What would you do if you didn't have to do it perfectly?
5. Jealousy and Envy
6. As a kid, I missed the chance to…
7. Writing these pages has shown me that…

ps: treating myself like a precious object will make me strong!

Week Eight

1. Surviving loss.
2. Gain disguised as a loss…
3. Age and Time tell me…
4. Taking the next small step instead of skipping ahead!
5. I was told that creative people are…
6. I am a talented person and I have a right to be an artist!
7. Dream: In a perfect world, I would be…

Week Nine

1. Call yourself by the right name: a Spade's a Spade!
2. Where's Compassion?
3. Tell me about enthusiasm…
4. Your creative U-turn?
5. When facing an obstacle, can you hear the roar of a lion?
6. In the present tense, describe yourself at the height of your future power!
7. Your Artist Totem.

Week Ten

1. Self-Care and Self-Protection
2. Procrastinating loose-ends?
3. My creative dream before…
4. What about dry seasons?
5. Fame: if it hasn't happened yet, it won't happen!
6. Competition: that person you know!
7. Your happiness touchstones…

Week Eleven

1. I am a Creator: Acceptance & Autonomy
2. Is Creativity a spiritual practice?
3. Your (honest) changes during this process!
4. I will nurture myself by…
5. What's wrong with praise?
6. The Artist is a child and hence not serious.
7. My ritual as a Creator…

Week Twelve

1. Tell me about Faith in the Self…
2. Adventures don't begin until you get into the forest (Grateful Dead)
3. Relinquishing control…
4. Creativity begins in darkness.
5. What about the fears, the resistances, the anger about moving on?
6. Five people who really support you.
7. Can you commit to further creativity?

You don't have to follow all of the prompts I have given you. You know how it works, with the *#rebeltherapy*: you only do what is best for you. Still, I can tell you that I see a difference in my clients, the ones who write, and the ones who don't. And I can tell you that I wished someone told me about journalling and its process and how therapeutic it is, well before I discovered it by chance. I am a strong believer that if I knew about it years ago, my path would have been different, and definitely quicker. It is true, that here I am now with the things that I know and my experience and knowledge *because* I did what I did; and what I did, did not include journalling at the time. Still, I wish I did: I wish I learned to listen to myself earlier. I wish I recognised my desires well before. I wish I could have understood my pain and what I was missing. I wish I befriended myself earlier. I wish I had the opportunity to write: "everything is going to be ok", with that sentence coming from my soul, my mind, my Inner Voice and my hand, instead of reading it in someone else's book. I would have hurt less; I would have hurt fewer people.

Within *#rebeltherapy* you do what you think is best for you. And you can find what is best for you, what you want, what you feel, what you like within your process of writing. You can use your writing to observe the present, dream about the future, and address your past. You will notice default reactions, likes, and dislikes, patterns, use of language. There will be days you don't want to write at all and days you cannot seem to stop: write about them. Some days you will draw, write small, write in very large letters: write about them. Some days it is going to be colouring only, or glueing and sticking memorabilia, or cry over some words: write about that.

Allow the process.

Allow *you* to come to the surface to breathe[14].

If by any chance, you are going to therapy, you might decide to bring your journal with you. At the same time, I had clients who wrote and burned the pages every day. Others wrote, and then glued them together. Writing and expressing yourself is liberating, not easy, but it means also that you are creating. And for some people, this is the only real process of creation, they feel allowed to embark on.

Now, some words of caution (as per usual):

1. You don't have to do it;

2. You don't have to show it to anyone;

3. If you want others to read your journal, ask yourself why: are you scared to say certain things and hence you hope for someone to "casually find" your journal, read it, and hence be aware of what you feel? This is *not* the reason to write your journal; also, it would not be a

---

[14] I could write for hours about the process of writing: which language do you write in, if you are bilingual? Which words do you prefer to use? Do you fill the whole page, do you test various pens? Do you have a preference for a specific type of paper, or brand of pens? Having studied some linguistic and glottology back in the days, I am fascinated by the spoken vs. the unspoken vs. the written both in therapy and in life in general. If you are bilingual, do you have a "language of the soul" or a "language of pain" you prefer to use? If you were to go to therapy, which language would you use? I would love to be able to explore this! If I were to say: *My mother was an alcoholic*, or *Mia madre era un'alcolista*, would it make any difference on the depth of my own self-development and therapeutic work?

process of growth and someone might argue that it is also not fair on the other person;

4. Hence, please remember the scope of writing your journal: explore and self-develop. Please, use it wisely;

5. If you think that you don't have enough privacy at home to write your journal, you might decide to find another place: a café, the library, or on the train, at a museum. I had clients who wrote at lunchtime in their vans;

6. If you decide to glue, stick, colour, paint, or burn the pages: please, be cautious of what, when, and how you are doing it;

7. Some people swear by typing, instead of long-hand writing. Or record themselves. All activities could be good, especially if we want to start the process. Still, there is a lot of literature that shows that physically writing long-hand on paper, and for 750 words circa per day, is more useful, productive, and therapeutic. It allows us to access certain parts of our brain which otherwise could be overseen if the words are typed on a laptop or on the phone, instead. There is again, a synergy, between brain, mind, hand, body, paper, time and pen/pencil/ink and creativity (gluing, sticking, drawing, sketching, connecting, doodling) which the faster act of typing, or voice recording, does not allow[15].

Again, as per everything in this book, try it. You don't have to become writers or artists if you don't want to. Or you might discover

---

[15] See for example *Handwriting: A complete Guide to Instruction Teaching Physical Patterns for Reading and Writing Fluency*, by C.H. Trafford and R.H. Nelson, Motor Science Consultants, just to mention one.

that the act of creating yourself, your new life, freeing yourself from the cage of your anxiety and emotional pain, will go hand-in-hand with an artistic creative process (ps: who are we kidding? It normally does). At that point, the act of journalling will assist you in channelling, gathering, describing, narrowing, planning, directing, guiding, and experimenting, with whatever creative activity you want to pursue[16].

And now for something else, which might help you.

I would like for you to try meditation if you haven't done it yet. I am not talking about guided meditation, the one to help you sleep, or to reduce your anxiety. I am simply talking about sitting there, comfortable, closing your eyes, and staying.[17]

---

[16] Please, for more information, have also a look at : https://www.theguardian.com/lifeandstyle/2014/oct/03/morning-pages-change-your-life-oliver-burkeman; the 750 Word online project at http://750words.com/ and finally a YouTube blogger I followed during my first experience: you can find Colin Druker here https://www.youtube.com/playlist?list=PLM5tamdRSllD8PD09Oj3EjvE6qpQUI_Lk

[17] For more information regarding various types of meditation, please look at: One-Moment Meditation at https://www.youtube.com/watch?v=F6eFFCi12v8; Loving-Kindness Meditation at https://www.mettainstitute.org/mettameditation.html; Zazen Meditation at http://www.zen-buddhism.net/practice/zen-meditation.html; the beautifully made event (and also totally free) that is the Deepak Chopra and Oprah Winfrey 21-day Free Meditation Experience that can be found at https://chopracentermeditation.com; also, if you are interested in a more theoretical approach to mindfulness, may I suggest you have a look at course at https://www.coursera.org/learn/mindfulness : "this innovative course combines conventional scholarly inquiry from multiple disciplines (ranging from psychology, through philosophy, to politics) with experiential learning (including specially designed 'meditation labs,' in which you'll get chance to practice and analyse mindfulness on yourself). [...] the course aims to provide a responsible, comprehensive, and inclusive education about (and in) mindfulness as a contemporary phenomenon."

Breathe in, breathe out. At the beginning try to concentrate on the air that goes in and out of your nose, or your lips. Some people might find counting helpful. Count one to ten, and if you feel that your mind wanders, start again, one to ten. And then start again. And start again. Sit there, for 10 minutes to start with and see what comes up. Let your thoughts come and go, observe them. Just think "oh, another thought": don't judge them. Don't think that you shouldn't think, don't oblige yourself to empty the mind, or to repeat some obscure mantras in an unknown language.

Just stay. Learn to stay.

Listen to your breath and your heart. And your muscles. Is there tension somewhere? You can move. Or you might decide to stay there a bit longer and see if you can live with that tension. Is there emotional pain somewhere? Do you feel any discomfort? Anxiety? Where is it coming from? What is it telling you? Does your mind go back, obsessively, to a particular topic? Something that you can't shake off for now?

What is the topic telling you?

What is the act of obsessing over this topic, telling you?

Do you find that you often obsess over different things in turn?

Do you like obsessing?

Is obsessing a reaction, an action, a distraction, or a destruction, for you?

What else could you be doing, or thinking about, instead of obsessing?

Is it important, for you, to find a solution to your problems?

Or, can you sit there, and simply *stay*?

You can try, of course, different types of meditation: autogenous training, body scanning, Metta meditation, Zazen, specific religious meditations depending on your beliefs. You can use CD's, or YouTube videos to assist you. You can buy books and record your own voice, to lead you into meditation. You can do it alone, or with other people. The options are almost infinite.

I simply like sitting, closing my eyes, and letting it be. Let it arise and try to love whatever comes. Then, of course, I journal about it. This is the reason why to me, those two are the essential practices which should go hand-in-hand on your path. Listen, feel, observe and write about it. You can buy books on both of the practices, go to a seminar, participate in conferences, watch videos on YouTube, and listen to podcasts. *None* of the above activities are substitutes for the practice.

Reading about meditation is not meditating.

Knowing about journalling and its therapeutic value is not journalling.

Saying "I know I should" doesn't help, either.

Reading the words I have just written, and maybe do a Google search, is not meditating nor journalling.

I remember that I was feeling under a lot of stress about a year ago and I so wanted to go and try some Zen meditation, as the one described by Thich Nhat Hanh: sitting for three hours, in silence, safe among likeminded people. My mind was, at the time, in a lot of chatter and I was craving for silence and that feeling of holiness some eastern practices seem to provide. So, off I went. I sat in this circle, the woman leading had a very soothing voice and I was just so happy thinking that I found my place. And then we started.

I think my mind lasted one minute. I had the first minute of peace. Then, as an avalanche, my mind vomited all sorts of stuff that she was hiding in some recesses. In my mind, I was complaining about everything and nothing. Nothing was ok. Everything was bad: the woman breathing next to me, the other one scratching herself, my back, my hair, the temperature; I felt hungry and thirsty. I was wondering if I would have fallen asleep, collapsed, while being watched by the other women, and judged. What if my stomach started to rumble? What if I farted? What was that song I was listening to the other day? That singer… the one who married… Gosh, what was her name?

...

I think that all of that must have happened in a fraction of a minute. I endured three hours, of sitting and walking meditation.

During the walking, I couldn't focus on anything else but the bad (for me) choice of colours of socks worn by the woman walking in front of me. I was angry, bitter, resentful, annoyed, emotionally drained, and there was a very loud voice inside me that was shouting "No no no no". Of course, I stayed and observed my mind at work. At times amused, but overall convinced that I had to try this experience in order to understand if it were for me, or not.

It wasn't.

But that doesn't mean that it might be, one day, the right practice for me on another stretch of my journey, some things and me being different.

So: try. Try different things and different opportunities for calming the mind. Explore. And observe.

Make it into an experiment. And, of course, write your findings.

Books are uniquely portable magic.

[S. King – On Writing]

april is the cruellest month

Start with broadening.

You might not live now, like I did at the time, in a tiny village up in the mountains. It was the late seventies and early eighties: the Berlin Wall was still standing, South Africa had apartheid; there were no phone, no pc's, and no internet.

My parents, regardless of their addiction, gave me the greatest gift any person could ever (and I really mean *ever*) give you: books and stories, because "literature is the study of humanity", says Daisaku Ikeda[18]

Here I want to list some of the ones I read, and I believe made me the person I am today. You don't have, again, to follow my same journey, but I do hope that among some of these, you might find one, or two, that will inspire you, that will broaden your horizon if need be; a mentor and a friend between words and ink. I am old school, and I do not apologise for it: I like books on paper, I like the smell of ink, I like to underline, fold the pages, write notes on the side. I like to open my bag and find a book in there. I like to hand them over, pass them on, and forget them on purpose in specific places[19]. The almost sensual and very tactile experience of reading is closer to bliss than almost no

---

[18] Ikeda, YOUTH, p.197

[19] Emma Watson has launched the project *Book Fairies* where, to encourage people to read, books are left in public places for people to enjoy. She has also founded her own book club, *Our Shared Shelf*, which can be access via her Instagram pages @emmawatson and @ourSharedshelf

other. If you have never immersed and lost yourself in a story, try it. Take your time, slow down, find a quiet and comfortable place, and let some words of old take you to faraway places.

Here are some of my all-time favourite:

- 1984 – George Orwell
- A Room of One's Own – Virginia Woolf
- Alice's Adventure in Wonderland – Lewis Carroll
- De Profundis – Oscar Wilde
- Eat, Pray, Love – Elizabeth Gilbert
- For Whom the Bell Tolls – Ernest Hemingway
- Foucault's Pendulum – Umberto Eco
- Heart of Darkness – Joseph Conrad
- Jane Eyre – Charlotte Bronte
- Jonathan Livingstone Seagull, a story – Richard Bach
- Life of Pi – Yann Martel
- Little Women and Good Wives – Louise May Alcott
- Lord of the Flies – William Golding
- M Train – Patti Smith
- Macbeth – William Shakespeare
- Matilda – Rohl Dahl
- Moby Dick – Herman Melville
- Nausea – Jean Paul Sartre
- One Hundred Years of Solitude – Gabriel García Márquez
- One, No One, One Hundred Thousand – Luigi Pirandello

- Pippi Longstocking – Astrid Lindgren
- Possession – A. S. Byatt
- Pride and Prejudice – Jane Austen
- Rebecca – Daphne Du Maurier
- Siddharta - Herman Hesse
- Skellig – David Almond
- The Baron in the Trees – Italo Calvino
- The Caretaker – Harold Pinter
- The Catcher in the Rye – J. D. Salinger
- The Grass is Singing – Doris Lessing
- The Graveyard Book – Neil Gaiman
- The Iron Man – Ted Hughes
- The Little Prince – Antoine de Saint-Exupéry
- The Magus – John Fowles
- The Spider's Web – Joseph Roth
- The Waste Land – T.S. Eliot
- The Wonderful Wizard of Oz – L. Frank Baum
- Ulysses – James Joyce

… and many others.

Do you have a favourite story? Which are your preferred ones, and why? Where do you find inspiration and support? What are you looking for in a book? And, what is it that you don't find in a book and that you think you need?

Can you re-write your own story?

No fact
speaks louder
than transforming our life circumstances.
No proof
is more powerful
than changing our destiny.
[Daisaku Ikeda]

nuns in town

Start with what you know.

When I was 16, one night I came home from school and I remember finding my father in the hall, smoking another cigarette, and as per usual Mother was in the bedroom. I told him that I understood, I mean, she was feeling poorly, she was sick, she had her migraines.

He looked at me and simply said: *She is pissed, Matilde. She is pissed. She has always been drunk. This is your mother, she has always been drunk.*

I never thought… I never knew… I took it for granted that every time Mother was in bed, once every 4 or 6 months (and for a whole month), it was because of her migraines. Nothing more. What do you mean drunk, pissed? Mother? No!

I didn't say a word. I left, went to a bar and I only remember shivering, and feeling like if my head was on a cold anvil and someone was banging a hammer on it, repeatedly; I recall probably my first experience of tunnel vision, and the *dread*, fear, the terror of going back home, and face the whole situation. My future was ruined, my plans were destroyed, I felt numb and very lonely.

Of course, I knew. I always knew. My parents were arguing, fighting, and shouting every night. Some of my first memories were of me hoping for them to get a divorce, to split up, and for someone to come and save me, take me away, hug me and love me. At any family reunion, I was extremely happy until relatives were starting to go back to their homes leaving me behind, and I would get into desperate tantrums throwing myself on the floor, begging, pleading to be taken away, not to be left there[20]. I don't remember being with adults that made me feel safe, nor I remember friends. I do not know what I was doing every day after school.

I remember being kicked, very hard, by my father and sent to eat a very cold soup, kneeling in front of the toilet seat, while Mother laughed. Everybody laughed when we remembered the episode: so funny! I didn't touch the floor! I was a naughty girl, I wasn't eating my food: so that same soup was taken out of the fridge, all cold and already fermenting, with big chunks of vegetables floating on some opalescent liquid and placed in front of me on the toilet seat. I had to kneel and eat that, or nothing else was served. When I was about 5 I remember my father coming home, checking my homework and how I was learning to trace the letters; if I managed to do it properly, you see; if he didn't like what he saw, he would tear all the pages and I had to start again. He kept on checking my progression in education till I went to University, almost interviewing me every night on what I had learned and studied unless of course, he was drunk.

Still, some of the evenings I spent with him learning maths and physics in the kitchen while the dishwasher was going, and mum was watching TV, were the best I had, even if he taught me logarithms and integers when I was only 14, and he kept on calling me *testona* (thick and

---

[20] I have never explored this, but even when very young and during these tantrums and desperation, a sort of external adult part of me *was watching* and *aware* it wasn't right that a little girl should feel this amount of pain.

stubborn, blockhead) while repeating it in a very strong patronising accent and banging his knuckle on my forehead. Otherwise, I remember him repeating incessantly: *think, think, think!*

I didn't want to think. I wanted to have a "normal" teenage life. Instead, I felt that I wasn't listened to nor understood. Already by the age of 10, I was planning to move away, (i.e. to live by myself upstairs in the loft), to get a job, pay the bills, and still finish school. I knew I could have walked to "work", but this situation would have only lasted for 4 years because after I would have had a motorbike, and things would have been easier. That was my plan at age 10.

I was *so old*, an old little lady, trapped in the body of a very thin, pale, and fragile girl. My father chose my school, my mother chose my clothes. I felt trapped. I had no friends, nor after-school activities. I was lonely most of the time.

What happened to me, to our family? Why was I always so miserable? One thing that I cherished, at that time, was silence. I invented words and entire languages, I had imaginary friends, who were actually more clients than friends, whom I would translate to from one imaginary language to another while sitting in the dark on an old trunk. I was also celebrating Mass to my dolls, a mock-up of a Bishop dressed in Mother's pink and white polka dots summer nightgown and using dad's Latin dictionaries as missals and the silver canteen I moved from the living-room into my bedroom.

And I was drawing nuns: nuns walking up a hill, nuns at the beach, nuns' in town, nuns everywhere. Plenty of nuns. Nuns made me happy.

At my secondary school run by Salesian priests, mass, hymns, God, incense-smelling handouts, songs in C-major and hushed black leather shoes and rubber soles felt safe and comforting. Yes, I could have become a nun: a silent order, please. A little cell, books and prayers, some soup at lunch and a garden where to stroll and contemplate. And silence, loads of silence. I could have settled for that bucolic life.

Instead, I barely remember what happened after that night at 16; and what happened before. Just pain. Just sadness. Just despair.

How can I not remember anything happy, some laughter, a smile, or hugs?[21]

Maybe I recollect a day in October 1975, walking in a field with mum and dad. I catch my left little finger into something, and dad has to cut the whole nail off there and then, and I don't cry: I am a good girl. My mother then agrees to take me the following day to buy a doll, a doll I can choose: Oh, Filomena, how much I loved you! I made sure that every night I would give you the same amount of attention I gave Marco the teddy bear and "that other doll I never gave a name to and I didn't like, and I felt very guilty about it". One caress each, one kiss

---

[21] I am sitting in a library this evening, proof-reading. I have an image, right in front of me. I must be 4 or 5. I have a light blue sort of apron, sewn by Auntie Bice and a matching heavy cotton little bag, which contains a pair of slippers. I must be at a pre-school, or still at nursery. I remember that mum stitched yellow felt ducks on all my belongings, as my personal symbol. I am standing up in front of a row of hangers, well higher than me. I climb onto a stool and I can see my hands, my tiny hands, hanging this little bag. I see my hands. I am me. I don't see myself from the outside. I smell overcooked little macaroni pasta, greasy and with plenty of cheese.

I am in Preston now, and I can only feel a violent surge of vomit, together with fear.

each. But you knew, and I knew, that I loved you more than anything and anybody else, my Filomena[22].

So much so that in the afternoon of May 6th, 1976 I asked dad to go back upstairs so that I could hide you under the desk, because I had a "strange feeling".

The memories of that day and of the following months are a big blur with a handful of extremely clear and vivid moments.

Dad came to pick me up from school (I was only 8) and he took me to lunch where he was working, at the army station in Gemona. We had a steak with some tomato sauce and capers… yak! Mum and sister (who at the time was almost 3) were away in the nearby city. Dad and I had lunch and, on the way out, he noticed that the lilies near the pond, which were of a bright yellow and violet, and thriving before lunch, were now all dead. Dad mentioned death, endings, sadness. I remember him being puzzled and questioning a lot. There was a lot of talking to himself. A sort of cape of doom came over me and I didn't know what to do with it. I think I smelled fear, like an animal. I didn't like what I was feeling. We went home, got changed and before leaving by car, I

---

[22] It's incredible how, even though I am sitting at the Library at Salford University, at my laptop and sipping a coffee at the age of 50, I can still smell her, and feel her in my arms. And I miss her, I feel moved to tears, in this room, among all these students, reminiscing an object I held 42 years ago. Part of me is almost reliving that same experience; and I have to remind myself that I am safe, here, where I am now, where I am sitting, and in my body. That those are things from the past. And they still hurt. Not having had kids, I cannot imagine the pain a Mother feels at losing one of hers, if I feel so much pain for a doll now.
Breathe in, breathe out.

asked dad to go back upstairs, to our flat, so that I could hide Filomena under my desk. We drove to Udine to meet mum and sister, went shopping for dad's new uniforms and hat, and then we all went for dinner with grandad and uncle to a restaurant that often saw us dining there: *Al Lepre*. I was sitting near grandad, at his right, eating spaghetti with homemade stewed veal sauce and I remember looking at him when the first seism happened. People shouted and automatically stood up. Noise of chairs and voices, cacophony and screams. Cries.

And then, deafening silence.

Waiting. Still. Is that it?

Then the second earthquake arrived[23].

People rushed out of the restaurant and I remember my grandad telling me not to worry and to continue eating.

How did I end up outside among the tiles falling from the roof, next to my mother holding her napkin and a fork, and questioning why she didn't take her bag?

6 May 1976, 9 pm. Another date, another unexpected change in my life. I don't how I felt at the time, all the time. Dad left to go back to the town (which didn't exist anymore) and help, being in the Army His

---

[23] The earthquake had a magnitude of 6.5 and a Mercalli intensity of X (as Extreme). Up to 990 people were killed, 2,400 were injured, and 157,000 were left homeless. Seventy-seven villages in the Friuli region were affected. There were many aftershocks, especially for two other earthquakes: one on 11th September of 5.6, and the second one again on 15th September same year of 6.0. 45 town were described as 'razed to the ground', another 40 as 'seriously damaged', and another 52 as 'simply damaged'.

hair turned grey overnight. Mum cried most of the time and she was left with no house, no belongings, and two young daughters, and sent to live with two old aunties. It was *camping*, but worse than camping, for a very long time. It was helicopters, cries, sirens, hospitals, death bulletins, gruesome story-telling, fake heroism, adventure and happy endings. It was pain. It was solitude. It was not having a place to stay and a safe family to support me. It was the final Russian roulette scene in *The Deer Hunter* over and over again. I seem to have only four vivid memories of that period.

The first one is right after the event, while dad was still in town and we were evacuated in the city: I remember one night I was sitting on a footstool, my back against the big wood stove in bright orange majolica in the aunties' dining room and I could see just the legs of mum, Auntie Anna, and Auntie Bice when sitting around the table. Maybe Uncle Piero was there, too. A large light blue citizen band radio was towering in the middle of the table and voices from another world were coming out. There were screams, shouting, swearing and a lot of cursing. We were trying to contact dad. The light in the dining room was orange-tinted due to a Venetian glass lamp shade. You could physically cut the air. Via that radio we were participating with women who were crying for their children, men crying for their wives, doctors, and helpers crying for a missing God who was nowhere to be found. It was dark, it was merciless, and I shouldn't have been there, on that stool, in that room. Still, I remember thinking: life is more than that, they are obsessing over this pain now instead of letting it go. I am old, now, I am not a little girl, and I cannot say this to anyone because they would otherwise think I am crazy and they won't believe me. I am old, I have already lived and died. I am as old as the mountains. This is nothing; there is so much peace somewhere else.[24]

My second memory is still very painful. We had a house at the seaside and we moved there for the summer and early autumn since we did not have a house anymore. Me, mum and sister. Dad, of course, wasn't there. He was coming down, broken and defeated when it was possible. I think that I began hearing him shouting "no more kids" then, in his nightmares; a common theme until he died in 1995. It was there, one hot summer day, that he told me that Marina, my Marina Pedi, my best friend at the time, was dead. They were all dead, he told me, me as an 8-year old girl. He described to me the most disgusting, horrific, gruesome and terrifying details of dismembered bodies, and of pain, and of blood, and how it changes colour and smell with the passing of time. He told me of white worms as thick as finger feasting on and recycling flesh; he told me of plastic crates full of body parts: the crate full of left hands, the crate full of right hands; he told me of diseases and injections, of nurses who offered themselves as prostitutes

---

[24] This could have been just a "therapeutic resource" that we know children implement to overcome trauma. Still, sometimes I ask myself what it *really* was. And I have my doubts. "Children who claim to remember fragments of a past life are found in some countries. Various explanations have been put forward as to why the alleged memories develop, ranging from reincarnation to 'therapeutic resource'. [A] study puts to the test the role of some psychological characteristics and the circumstances in which the children live, such as fantasy, suggestibility, social isolation, dissociation, and attention-seeking. [...] There was some evidence of post-traumatic stress disorder-like symptoms. Eighty per cent of the children [observed] spoke of past-life memories of circumstances leading to a violent death (mostly accidents, also war-related deaths and murder). It is discussed if this imagery - when experienced repeatedly - may serve as a stressor." Please, see https://www.ncbi.nlm.nih.gov/pubmed/12689435

to the aides; of men who lost their minds and wondered at night looking for their homes; of songs hummed all together, of soup, of people surviving on wine; of cows crying every night; of heat, and communality; of the communists from Yugoslavia, and the professionals from Germany, and the politicians from Rome; of how people were then substituting documents and disappeared pretending to be dead, of butcheries that no one would have questioned thanks to the quake; of pick axes found in people's backs.

He told me of his platoon, all dead; his military legacy, dead; all of them, in the barracks, and of their mothers screaming.

And he told me of how I survived; because of my year and my class, there was no one else left.

I survived. The others were all dead.[25]

I don't remember how I spent the rest of the summer and the beginning of autumn. I remember going back to school in September in a makeshift building with new teachers, new students, new books in another town. With other survivors. I am wondering now: where are they? How are they doing? Then, we moved to a village in the mountains where I scared my parents by sleeping for three full days, waking up only to eat a couple of biscuits. The doctors told my mother that it must have been because of the shock. Something inside me shut

---

[25] As I am writing these words, just as a reminder from the Universe, again at the beginning of May, a very hot month, there is another earthquake in the same area. I read the newspapers and I can only remind myself to breathe. And chant.

down and I needed to sleep. Also, one of my breasts grew particularly large, while I remember planning in my mind to blow up friends' houses if they didn't invite me to their birthdays. We got a dog, Kira, but unfortunately, she didn't last long, and I was still basically extremely sad. Existentially sad. I couldn't understand, and no one explained. I cannot believe that *never*, in all the years of therapy my parents went through because of their addiction, no one has ever mentioned the earthquake and what that might have meant for a whole generation.

Then, my fourth detailed memory, is me being in another home, at the kitchen sink, washing glasses and feeling another small quake and seeing the glasses moving and clanging, and ringing and banging against each other. I simply could not stop laughing. That was the funniest thing ever. I swear.

After that, not much to report till that night at 16. The year after I had surgery, which scared me and made me question life, and death, and survival. Again. My surgery was for two dermoid cysts: these are created from embryonic cells and are of a vanished twin. They found nails, hair, fingers, and other cells of a boy. My mother always wanted a boy, and she would have called him Martino, she told me after the surgery. She almost accused me of killing him.

I then won a scholarship for a two-year course in the UK in a fairly exclusive international college, and when I finished and was summoned back home, I only lasted a year. Then, the panic attack.

Still, somehow, I managed to get married and I also succeeded in not finishing university.

My father passed away at the age of 56 when I was only 26. The last words I heard him saying were a repeated "*if only*": if only I chose to…, if only I decided to… if only I said… I cannot imagine his pain and the regrets he had in life. Was I also one of them? Still, how sad his life must have felt: dying at 56, without accomplishing what he really wanted to do, which probably now, in hindsight, was to be free and happy and to follow his dreams. Still, I miss him to this day.

I then felt so much hatred for being stuck with Mother: she was loud, excessive, a depressed alcoholic. She emotionally blackmailed me since I can remember: I should have died when I was born, I was a failure, I would never accomplish anything, she knew better than me what I needed; I should have helped, always, and repeatedly simply because she gave me life; and because she paid for my education; and because she paid for my food; and clothing; and for heating and electricity. I should have gone to her house whenever she called, even during my honeymoon, while she threatened me over the phone that if I didn't run to help her, she would have killed herself, and then I would be cursed.

Of course, I run.

I run every time she called. I run even when she did not call because at times I was afraid of the silences; at other times I just wanted to enjoy her when she was happy. I run, and called, and helped, and cleaned, and even bought alcohol and gave her diazepam when I perfectly knew she shouldn't have taken it. I was way too scared to say No. I blamed her for my shitty life, for the breaking up of my marriage, for me losing so many jobs I lost the count, for my fears, for my losing weight, for missing out in life, for staying at home when I could have left. I blamed her for everything. If leaving her and not answering the phone were so easy, there would be no domestic violence, no abuse. Instead we, the abused, keep on going back.

Still, I kept my mouth shut and loved her. I really thought I was helping her. I protected and justified her as much as I could. I still do, somehow. I do miss her, to this day.

During those years, when I was trying to find myself again, I made mistakes, and I hurt people. It is very easy to say that hurt people, hurt people, but it is true. I did things which were not right and looked for belonging where I shouldn't have had. Or maybe, I did really need to go *there* to do what I did. I only know that I suffered, and other people suffered. Because of this, I admitted my fault, I was held accountable, and I did pay my dues. I also decided that I had to change.

Around 2007 my mother was more depressed and in a drunken stupor, than serene and sober. She basically tried to kill herself consistently almost every month. Then, it became every week. I was feeling drained, tired, and sad; I really gave up. I walked out of my marriage, lost my job, and with no money whatsoever rented a room. I was lying to everybody: to my mother that I still had a job so that I could disappear for part of the day; to my husband that sooner or later I would go back home.

One night, one of those countless "another night" in hospital, with my mother, even the doctor in AE begged me not to save her: "Next time, he told me, just let her go".

I had a client once, who told me that sometimes she still calls her abuser, just to hear his voice and not to feel alone, in the world. Until he is alive and shouts at her, she is not lonely. She reminded me so much of myself.

How could I let her go? She was my mother! Do I have to turn a blind eye and not run to help her, clean her, wash her, justify her, save her? I felt not understood: no one was helping me, it was like shouting at a brick wall: the hospital wouldn't keep her there for longer to help me, the church wouldn't help, nor there's anything like social care in Italy. Nothing. I was alone. And no one was supporting me.

One night, *that* night, driving home from the hospital, I thought that I only had two options: killing my mother, and be free, or killing myself, and be free. I did not see any other option for me. I only knew I could not go on like that.

I was driving home, it was about 2 am, in July, a very warm night. I didn't even remember when was the last time that I had eaten something. I just smoked, and drunk coffees with loads of sugar. I shaved my head a couple of weeks before and I lost so much weight you could see most of my bones. Still, I wasn't stopping. I was marching.

But that night, on that road, I really thought that was it. I left her in hospital, she was taken care of for that night. The sky was clear, the cicadas were singing, I had one last fag while driving, and saw a big truck coming the other way.

It was very easy, it would have been so easy. I felt so tired, and lonely, and exhausted. I just wanted this "stuckness" to end.

But I couldn't do it.

I steered the car away from the truck and I chose a third option I never actually thought of before: to leave.

I realised that night that I had done enough. There was nothing else I could have done to save her, but I still had time to save me.

I don't even know how things unfolded. I only know that Stefania helped me find a job in the UK, Cesare paid for my flight, Nicoletta helped me to pack my belonging, and Giovanni drove me to the airport.

It was the 4th of August 2008, I was 40 and I was leaving with only 20 euros in my wallet.

And once the storm is over,
you won't remember how you made it through,
how you managed to survive.
You won't even be sure,
whether the storm is really over.
But one thing is certain.
When you come out of the storm,
you won't be the same person who walked in.
That's what this storm's all about.

[Haruki Murakami]

me, them and an empty chair.

One of the first things that I did as soon as I moved to the UK was to fall in love with someone. Now I know that I simply substituted my Mother with him. Because Mother died in March 2009. She died in her house, at 3 am, while going upstairs to bed. She died on the stairs. I can't imagine what her last thoughts must have been: did she realise that she was dying? Did she know that her daughters were not there? Did she want me there? Would I have run if she called me?

I heard of her death by a message in my answer phone, because I was too much of a coward to answer the phone when I saw her name on the display; and then too guilty for not answering the phone. So, I listen to the message instead. "Matilde, this is Marco, I am sorry to tell you that…" For a long period of time, after her death and her solitary funeral, I almost "turned into her". It wasn't just empathising, in was morphing into her body language, her voice, her mannerism. What was the very last instant of her consciousness?

I never felt any guilt for leaving Italy and leaving her behind. I knew then as much as I know now that, at the time, there was nothing else I could have done. It is different now: with what I know, and with the people I work with, and the typology of my clients which keep on coming, and coming, and coming. I feel I *could* do something now. But not then. Our last day together was her funeral: her and I. The two of us. I drove her ashes to the cemetery via the scenic route, and we stopped in front of her house, her school, the beach. I told her about my new life. I bought her favourite flowers. I took her to have lunch with me in a little restaurant next to cemetery. Then the priest arrived, blessed the wooden box. I handed her over. Turned and felt like fainting. No one was there. Not one.

Working with people in recovery is like trying to save my mother and father all over again. Is it wrong? This is probably my motivation or my karma. I know that my clients are not Mother and Father. I know that their stories are different. They are my inspiration to go and sit in front of these people, though.

I feel a sense of peace, now, when I think about them. My first wonderful English boyfriend, the substitute for my controlling mother, broke up with me and it was brutal. At the time, I was fortunate enough to recognise that the pain and anger and rage and anxiety I was feeling, and in such powerful waves, were not because of him. Don't get me wrong, he played his part in being *him* (but I could not have found any different since I was who I was). My reactions were so intense because I was experiencing abandonment and rejection, all over again.

One evening after college, fresh of a couple of weeks of Gestalt, I sat in front of an empty chair. Admittedly, I first opened a bottle of wine, and then I went on a massive rant. I imagined *him* sitting there. Then my Mother showed up, very loud and accusing and blackmailing me. Then my Father sat there, silently angry and patronising, his leg with that constant twitch. I attacked everybody, I blamed everybody, I cried, I shouted, I argued, I vomited words of accusation; tears, snot and all.

And then, as by magic, I let them all go. I just forgave them all. I recognised their agony, I embraced my pain and accepted my need to move on. Do I still miss my parents, every day? I am not so sure. Now I can remember some good times, and the lessons learned. My Buddhist practice helped me in understanding my pain. It helps me in defining a clear boundary between me and my abusers because I want to move on in life. Blaming them for the rest of my life does not help them and does not serve me. Blaming is a pointless game, where no one wins. In this book you will not find their stories because it feels like a tedious game: I know they accused their parents, who in turn accused their parents and the war, and who in turn accused probably another war, and the lack of education, and their parents! If we keep on going back blaming and accusing and faulting everybody else in the past, sooner or later we reach God, and we blame him. What is the point? This blame game has to stop somewhere. It might as well end with me.

When I look back, I can only see an incredible journey, "A journey from growing clarity, understanding, and healing" (Eldredge). And then I realized that what I thought was healing, was nothing more than *relief*.

I think that healing is what I am learning to experience now.

Five years ago, thinking I knew everything, I was still in a job I was not enjoying but it was paying my bills, *him* was about to leave and still the bottom line of my life was ruled by "I need to find someone; even though I am a strong woman, I need to fall in Love and my Man needs to tick loads of boxes; even though I am Independent, where is this Man who will unconditionally love, rescue and save me? And even though I am very open-minded, my man-shopping-list is long and very detailed" and *bla bla bla*...

Where was I in all of this? Which, funnily enough, is a question I often ask my clients: *where are you, in all of this?*

What was I prepared to do, in order not be alone? The message I received from my parents was "if you don't do exactly what I want you to do, I won't love you anymore, and you can figure out for yourself what that might mean. It means, of course, abandonment and death." (Scott Peck)

My next step was not forward, back backwards. I looked at my parents together with a theory that could justify, explain, and provide change; which of course led me nowhere since they were both gone. I decided to be strong and bought myself a couple of books which deal with alcoholism and children of alcoholics; in Geringer Woititz I learned that ACA's (Adult Children of Alcoholics) can only guess what *normal* means and seek constant attention and appreciation; who are extremely loyal, but also super-responsible; and that we take each other very seriously. They were describing me!

It was not until I read Robert Ackerman's *Perfect Daughters* that my eyes opened, and I could make full sense of what happened in the past. Ackerman, borrowing from Erikson, explains that there are 8 stages in the psychological development of a child, and each one is a prerequisite for the next one. Normally children of alcoholics (and especially daughters of alcoholic fathers) do not even have the possibility of learning the first lesson, which is to trust.

If a child does not learn trust from a trustworthy parent, how can she trust others in adult life? And how can she trust herself? Hence, all the other lessons in life are never understood: learning how to be autonomous vs inadequate and worthless; the balance between rules and inconsistency; being valuable vs. unlovable – always second to drinking and whatever I did was never enough; discovering my identity vs "I need somewhere to belong"; learning the difference between intimacy and "giving myself away to gain affection", to mention just a few.

I had to start again to learn as a child does, all these stages while at the same time accepting any *defeat* with the "grace" of an adult woman; although inside I might still feel the grief of me-child, of little Matilde.

My challenge since then has been to become my healthy role model. I understood reading Lee Cori's *The Emotionally Absent Mother* that I have to take care of myself as my too-drunk mother never did.

The lesson learned is that the kind of love I have been given was "I love you but let me do my own things (mostly drinking). If you want to stay, sit there and be quiet". It was like living in a private echo chamber all the time, with the fear of what will I find when I get home, behind that door? Will it be happiness, tears, laughter, shouting, a surprise? Or silence? This uncontrollable situation led me to a desperate need for stability, even if stability meant living with a controlling and abusive partner. But at least *it is the same shit that I know so well, every day*. I simply grew accustomed to those some-ones who defined *reality* for me.

The only way to make sense of all this, for me, meant taking charge.

From Marion Woodman I learned that "individuals tend to repeat the pattern of their own actual birth every time life requires them to move onto a new level of awareness": when there is addiction, children tend to avoid facing reality; from Anne Dickson I learned that "an assertive approach offers an effective alternative by showing a way to combine care and respect for another person without losing sight of [my] own needs and wishes" and also how to draw comfort from separateness.

Therefore, I started making little moves. Instead of staying at home I went out, visiting places; I took myself on holiday, to Scotland; I even took myself out for dinner one Saturday. I wanted to learn the difference between *alone* and *lonely*: I have felt very alone, but I am not that lonely now.

One day I met someone who asked me: *so, what brought you to England?* I automatically said: broken promises.

Broken Promises.

I won't drink again.

I will help you with your homework.

Not, now. Next time. Next Year. Next Summer.

I will come to pick you up after school.

I will come and talk to your teachers, wait for me there.

I promise... *te lo giuro...* I swear...

There have been other promises that I am happy I was the one to break: the I promise that I will be a failure in my life; that I would end up with nothing; and that I will always be worthless.

As I began to love myself,
I found that anguish
And emotional suffering
Are only warning signs
That I was living against
My own truth.
Today, I know,
This is Authenticity.

As I began to love myself,
I understood how much
It can offend somebody
As I try to force
My desires on this person,
Even though I knew
The time was not right
And the person was not ready for it,
And even though this person
Was me.
Today,
I call it Respect.

As I began to love myself,
I stopped craving for a different life,
And I could see
That everything
That surrounded me
Was inviting me to grow.
Today,
I call it Maturity.

As I began to love myself,
I understood
That at any circumstance,
I am in the right place
At the right time,
And everything happens
At the exactly right moment,
So I could be calm.

Today,
I call it Self-Confidence.

As I began to love myself,
I quit stealing my own time,
And I stopped
Designing huge projects
For the future.
Today, I only do
What brings me joy
And happiness,
Things I love to do
And that make my heart cheer,
And I do them in my own way
And in my own rhythm.
Today,
I call it Simplicity.

As I began to love myself,
I freed myself of anything
That is no good for my health
- Food, people, things, situations
And everything that drew me down
And away from myself.
At first I called this attitude
A healthy egoism.
Today,
I know it is Love of Oneself.

As I began to love myself,
I quit trying to always be right,
And ever since,
I was wrong
Less of the time.
Today,
I discovered that is Modesty.

As I began to love myself,
I refused to go on
Living in the past
And worry about the future.
Now, I only live for the moment,
Where everything is happening.
Today,
I live each day,
Day by day,
And I call it Fulfilment.

As I began to love myself,
I recognized that my mind
Can disturb me
And it can make me sick.
But, as I connected it to my heart,
My mind became a valuable ally.
Today,
I call this connection
Wisdom of the Heart.

We no longer need to fear arguments,
Confrontations or any kind of problems
With ourselves or others.
Even stars collide,
And out of their crashing
New worlds are born.
Today, I know...
That is Life.

[Charlie Chaplin]

hello, my name is Matilde and I am a Perfect Daughter

Women who grew up in an alcoholic home develop similar personality traits and characteristics. The following are hints, ideas, support that I personally found helpful and enlightening. Read this following with an open mind: maybe your parents are not in addiction, but there was still pain in your family; you are a son: what do you feel when reading the following? Do you recognise any sign? Please, read the books from Robert J. Ackerman and Robin Norwood about this subject, where I have taken the following.

Are you one of my sisters?

Fear of losing control: Perfect Daughters maintain control over their behaviour and feelings. They also try to control the behaviour and feelings of others. They do this because they are afraid not because they want to hurt themselves or others. They fear that if they relinquish control their lives will get worse, and they can become very anxious when they are not able to control a situation.

Fear of Emotions or Feelings: Perfect Daughters tend to bury their feelings (particularly anger and sadness) since childhood and are not able to feel or express emotions easily. Ultimately, they fear all-powerful emotions and even fear positive emotions like fun and joy.

Avoid conflict: Perfect Daughters have a fear of people, who are in authority, people who are angry and do not take personal criticism very well. Often, they misinterpret assertiveness for anger. Therefore, they are constantly seeking approval of others whilst losing their identities in the process. Frequently they isolate themselves.

A high burden of responsibility and constant approval seeking: Perfect Daughters are oversensitive to the needs of others. Their self-esteem comes from others' judgments of them, thus having the compulsive need to be perfectionists and be accepted.

An inability to relax and have fun: Perfect Daughters cannot have fun because it is stressful, especially when others are watching. The child inside is frightened, and in an effort to appear perfect, exercises strict self-control.

Harsh self-criticism and low self-esteem: Perfect Daughters are weighed down with a very low sense of self-esteem and respect, no matter how competent they may be.

Denial: Whenever Perfect Daughters feel threatened, they tend to deny that which provoke their fears.

Difficulties with intimacy: Perfect Daughters fear intimacy because it makes them feel that they lost control. They have difficulties expressing their needs and consequently have problems with their sexuality and repeat relationship patterns.

Develop a victim mentality: Perfect Daughters may either be passive or aggressive victims and are often attracted to others like them whether in friendships, career and love relationships.

Adopting compulsive behaviour: Perfect Daughters may eat compulsively or become workaholics. They may become addicted and co-dependent in a relationship or behave compulsively in other ways.

Sadly, they may abuse alcohol and become alcoholics like their parent(s).

More comfortable living in chaos or drama than in peace: Perfect Daughters become addicted to chaos and drama, which gives them their adrenaline fix and feelings of power and control.

The tendency to confuse love with pity: Perfect Daughters are often in relationships with people they can rescue.

Abandonment issues: Perfect Daughters will do anything to save a relationship, rather than face the pain of abandonment even if the relationship is unhealthy.

Tendency to see everything and everyone in extremes, when under pressure: Black or white, friends or enemies, madly in love or broken up just after an argument.

Physical illness: Perfect Daughters are highly susceptible to stress-related illnesses.

Suffering from an accumulation of grief: Perfect Daughters are frequently depressed. Losses experienced during their childhood were often never grieved for because the alcoholic family doesn't tolerate intensely uncomfortable feelings.

Overreaction to outside changes: Perfect Daughters remain hyper-vigilant, constantly scanning their surroundings for potential catastrophes.

Perfect Daughters Attracted to Compulsive Personalities: Many lose themselves in their relationship with others and sometimes find themselves attracted to alcoholics or other compulsive personalities - such as workaholics. They are generally attracted to those who are emotionally unavailable. Perfect Daughters sometimes like to be the "rescuer" and will form relationships with others who need their help, to the extent of neglecting their own needs. What happens is that they place the focus on the needs of someone else whilst not having to examine their own difficulties and shortcomings. Often, these Perfect Daughters will acquire the characteristics of alcoholics, even if they never drink themselves. They can be in denial, develop poor coping strategies, have an inability to problem solve and form dysfunctional relationships.

People affected by parental alcohol problems often share similar feelings. Some talk about:

1. feeling different from other people
2. difficulty making and maintaining intimate relationships
3. fearing rejection and abandonment, yet rejecting others
4. being loyal even when loyalty is undeserved
5. finding it difficult to have fun
6. judging themselves without mercy
7. fearing failure but sabotaging success
8. overreacting to changes over which they have no control
9. lying when it would be just as easy, to tell the truth
10. guessing at what 'normal' is

These issues can continue whether the parent is still drinking or not. And sometimes, when the parent, or partner, is not drinking anymore, we feel even worse because we seem to have lost our mission in life, or place, or identity.

Please, remember: You are not alone

What you can do

Find out more about alcohol and the effects on the family: understanding how alcohol affects the person drinking and everyone else in the family can help you to be in the best position to support someone who has or has had, an alcohol problem, and most importantly to look after yourself.

Join support groups, look for professional counselling; and/or commit to participating for example in sessions dedicated to the Perfect Daughters or any other family member; or to the Stages of Psychosocial-development as described by Erikson.

Remember you are not responsible for other people's drinking: you can't control someone else's drinking or behaviour. Pouring away, watering down, or hiding alcohol may make things worse, and the person may become angry, aggressive or secretive.

Remember your parent's drinking is not, and never was your fault.

Can we please read that sentence again, together?
Our parents' drinking is not, and never was our fault.

Remember (always!) the six Cs:

1. I didn't cause it
2. I can't control it
3. I can't cure it
4. I can take care of myself
5. I can communicate my feelings
6. I can make healthy choices

*The true measure of human beings
and of the depth and breadth of their lives
is found in their wisdom,
the beliefs and philosophy
from which that wisdom derives,
and to what extent they have embodied
or actualized their ideals.*

[Daisaku Ikeda]

recovery doesn't exist

Start Here.

During my experience with working in recovery from addiction and being a Perfect Daughter, I have often noticed how *recovery* could be compared to a planned journey by car.

You are in London, you get a second-hand car and decide to drive all the way to Edinburgh: you have never been there before and are feeling very excited.

Someone helped you to pack your bag and has been kind enough to give you even a map. They have travelled before, heading north; not really to Edinburgh, but *in that direction.*

You set off, it's early morning. You are excited! The M25 is busy and your journey is slow. You are not bothered nor worried. You have plenty of time. During your journey, you stop for a cup of coffee and to stretch your legs: maybe you also buy a CD. You get a bit bored sometimes and wonder: why am I going to Edinburgh?! Who chose that?! Could I have chosen somewhere else?! Maybe a different route, I could stop on the way, visit other places. What about making a detour to Glastonbury and have my future read? You feel lonely in the car, the station you have chosen plays always the same songs, sometimes it rains and then the sun comes out. Around Birmingham, the roadworks are really slowing you down; you also took the wrong turn and you now have to pay the toll. Then, you hit 'The North'.

Around Preston… *ppppppfffffs*! your car stops. It doesn't work. An abrupt stop. You can choose the damage.

What do you do? You argue with the car, blame your friend who suggested you bought *that* car, or you can blame the previous owner. No maps will help you there.

Why? Because you are an inexperienced driver. You haven't checked the tyres, the levels, the wind wipers; if there are spare light bulbs in the glove compartment. You are surrounded by other inexperienced drivers who know how to drive but have never been that far. They are on their journey, too. They haven't arrived yet. No one taught you to get a breakdown insurance. They gave you a map and a pat on the shoulder and off you went.

But, when in Preston, and your car does not move, what do you do? You will feel lonely and lost. Abandoned, and maybe resentful.

During your journey through recovery, you have been given a map, you wrote letters to your Self, the substance, maybe followed the 12 Steps; you spent time making long lists of wrongdoings and then other long lists of things you should be grateful for. You eat, breathe, live recovery together with people in recovery. People who are on the same journey and who also have got a map.

What about the initial checks? What about your sense of identity, your desire to belong, your needs? What about your dreams? What about working with someone who has been to Edinburgh, and beyond, before?

What if I told you that *addiction* does not exist. What if I told you that, consequently, also recovery does not exist. That is all in our head, in our heart, in our fears.

I have been working for the past years with people in recovery from addiction. Most of the time I do not even know their *drug* of choice, but it is ok because there is no difference.

Recovery is very easy: you just stop. You stop drinking, stop using, stop gambling, stop promiscuity. You just stop. You also stop *thinking* about it. Easy, isn't it? If only…

Addiction is a plaster we put on a cut that has already been infected, and that we don't want to address. We let the infection grow, it is smelly, and the more it hurts and the more it stinks, the more we cover it up with more bandages, creams, and more plasters.

> *wounds need air, to breathe, to heal.*
> *concealing your wounds with bandaids and bandages*
> *only slows down your healing.*
> *confront your wounds, bring them out in the open,*
> *ask them why they still hurt,*
> *ask them what they require to be soothed —*
> *ask your wounds important questions.*
> [billy chapata]

Take it off. Take it all off.

Look at that cut, clean that infection. Ask for help, for someone to assist you in the process. Then, say *thank you*, and move on. You will always have a scar, but there will be no infection anymore.

I hope that you recognise these words not as recovery, but as *discovery*. This whole book is not about recovery: it is a book about discovery. Recovery doesn't exist. Life is discovery - the journey into learning who you *really* are and what you *really* want under all those bandages and plasters; because no one can answer those questions for you.

I was watching a motivational video, the other day. A woman was providing the example of a car hitting a tree at 5 mph, which creates a certain type of damage, and comparing it to the same car hitting the same tree at 80 mph: a different kind of damage, both to the car and the driver. What is the solution? What would you choose?

Most people would choose to hit the tree at 5 mph, who wouldn't!

The point is: why not cutting down the tree?

Why not looking at your life and experiences from a different perspective?

You will probably have all heard the story about that woman who is walking along a river bank, looking for a way to cross to the other side. Finally, she sees someone on the opposite bank and shouts across "Hey, how do you get to the other side?"

The other person yells back at her "You already are on the other side!"

Many clients come to me and sooner or later the stereotypical sentence of "the light at the end of the tunnel" crops up. *I can see the light at the end of the tunnel, I don't know how long this tunnel is, I do not see any light at the end of the tunnel.*

My dear coach Bob Buckley puts it very elegantly when he says: there is no fucking tunnel.

> *"And now don't start clinging
> to the remedy,
> to the method.
> That temptation arises.
> It is the last temptation, the very last effort of the mind to survive."*
> [Osho]

Recovery, the opium of the people (thank you, K. Marx!): The opium, a drug. My past is not of an addict: I have never been an alcoholic and I have never used drugs. Or, haven't I?

Because I have been smoking cigarettes for most of my life until I quit.

Have I ever considered myself an addict, while smoking? Yes, always.

Do I consider myself an ex-addict now? No.

Do I label myself someone in recovery from nicotine addiction? Nope.

Do I have cravings now, do I ever want a fag? Yes, and no.

Let me put it bluntly and straightaway: it does not matter what you use, and it does not matter how much of it you are using. It is the *reason* that makes you an addict.

You can be using alcohol, drugs of any sort, porn, gambling, shopping, chocolate, compulsively scrolling your Facebook timeline, or playing *Candy Crush Saga*, or co-dependency: you are addicted to an emotion, the desire to disappear, to pretend everything is alright and that you are having an amazing time, and to stop the pain. You could be drinking one glass of wine only, and still, you won't go out of the house if you don't have that one glass: you are just employing different means to stop *that* pain, not to face *that* hurt, nor to feel *that* emotion. What you miss is a comforting sense of belonging, a sense of real identity, confidence, of knowing who you are and what the hell you are supposed to be doing on this planet, here, and now, with your life; or of being absolutely ok with not having a clue. That's the fear: that this whole journey you are doing is, in the end, pointless. And: why the fuck am I suffering so much? And: what have I done so wrong in my life to deserve this? And: this is it, it has always been like this, and nothing will ever change, and no one will ever come to change it (i.e. to help me), at least my [buddies] understand me.

Your [buddies] understand you because they feel the same pain, and they don't admit it even to themselves. So, next time you are drinking, shooting up, watching porn: think about the pain. For once. That's all I am asking: think about the pain and realise that 1. that pain is not going to go away by itself; 2. that pain is not going to kill you; 3. that you can change what you think and how you feel about the pain.

Therefore, what are you going to do about it? Not your family, your mates, the NHS, your friends, your therapist, your mentor, and sponsors, or me sitting in front of this keyboard now. What are *you* going to do about *your* pain?

And do you know why I am asking this question? Because you are in charge.

You are never powerless, impotent, ineffective, helpless, inadequate, defenceless, feeble, incapable, unable, incompetent, inept, weak and useless. Dirty.

Or, shall we talk about your new-found addiction, the recovery process, and the meetings? For how long do you want to be considered an ex-addict? For how long do you want to keep on celebrating your anniversaries? How many times do you want to stand up and introduce yourself as 'someone in recovery'?

Don't get me wrong, meetings are great: you meet people, you talk to people, people call you and text you, and it feels like a big family who understands you. You found a place to belong to; and your identity, the comfort of this uniqueness given by the label of an ex-addict, in recovery, an alcoholic. You found your little ghetto, where only people with the same experiences can enter, listen to you, give you advice, and support you. *Because they know.* That little comforting ghetto means that you will not trust anyone else; hence, that you will not grow. Your uniqueness will then disappear. You will discover that you can feel excitement for life only when you talk about the past and about when you were using: you learn the pleasure of pain. Like the excitement that some veterans feels remembering ambushes, battles, and the noise of machine guns.

Scared and hurt animals always return home: is this the life you want to live?

Like the prodigal son, should you ever relapse, they will be ready to take you back and offer you a brew. Maybe, you have decided even to give back to the community which has helped you so much.

Do you know how I call this *caritas*? Fear.

You were scared before, in addiction.

You are petrified now, in recovery, without the support of your shoji screen.

You will be terrified and resentful, next.

Let me ask you a question: has that pain gone away? Has your dream, as a little kid, always been to work in recovery? Oh, I can almost feel your grey cells coming up with all the *right justifications* of why you should be doing what you are doing: your kids, your family, because you have been a bad boy in the past or a bad girl; you are receiving so much now, you should give back and help others. Well, let me tell you: this is what will create frustration and resentment; and this is what is going to take you straight to relapsing: the word *should*. This probably means that you have learned nothing, and you have simply swapped addiction. Out with the drug, in with the meetings. Out with a partner, in with a new job, new house, another bottle of wine, a new car, a new phone, another holiday.

Are you may be thinking now that you should stop going to meetings straightaway, just because I told you so? Like, from this week? Or, never to go to any?

Go to your meeting and use them to find out who you really are.

Go to meetings, and for once listen to that little nagging voice within you: what is it saying?

Go to meetings, and to therapy.

Go to meetings, and back to college.

Go to meetings, and then one night don't go, without feeling "I *should* be going there".

Go to meetings, and change location.

Go to meetings and be a rebel: stand up and say "Hello, my name is XYZ and I am not powerless. I can actually tell you that I feel fully in charge of my faculties and I choose not to use."

Go to meetings, and when/if they ask you to pledge allegiance to a Higher Power, ask yourself where this HP is located. Do you need to be saved? Don't get me wrong: I am a believer and not a piece of Velcro following the bandwagon because I am desperately lonely and in pain.

The steps are not the solutions. Meetings are not the solutions.

{Philosophy, spirituality, and psychotherapy} all together work because only *change* works. Only learning to stay in a dark room by ourselves and our thoughts and our shadow, and our petty little mean secrets and pain and resentment and frustration helps.[26]

Growing up helps. Taking full responsibility helps.

Happiness does not help, because happiness is only a mood so stop chasing a mood.

You don't buy bread and milk only once in your life, don't you? You go out every day to buy them fresh. This is Life: you work on your mood and your commitment, your resolve, and you pain, and well-being every day. Determination and motivations are nothing more than simply reminding ourselves our destination, every day[27].

This is the same whether you are "in recovery", or not. Hence, recovery doesn't exist.

Take a step in a different direction and start looking for your Self.

For the ones who while reading all of the above could not stop thinking *"yes, but she is not an addict, she has never been one, she does not understand what it means, she doesn't get it, my life has been hell, you don't understand, my story is different, let me tell you what happened to me…"* and this is still your running commentary now: please, go to meetings. Please, know that there's nothing wrong with that. It's your journey, and I wish you all the happiness and support you can find.

---

[26] There is a very powerful and beautifully made video by the philosopher Alain de Botton about the concept of addiction. Please, watch it. You can find it here: https://youtu.be/f55QO2isoKM

[27] Thank you, Bob Buckley!

If instead, you want to know more about yourself and if you feel you are ready for that, if you want to hear a different point of view, if you want to try something diverse, and you want to push your boundaries and really change, for good: look, go out, search, explore. And journal about it.

Osho writes a little story the Buddha used to say, about 5 idiots carrying a boat over their head while walking through a village: "We cannot leave this boat that helped us to come from the other shore to this shore. How can we leave it. It is because of it that we have been able to come here. Without it, we would have died on the other shore. […] Do you think the boat is dangerous? It is dangerous if you are thinking about carrying it on your head for your whole life out of sheer gratitude; otherwise, it is just a raft to be used and discarded. All methods are rafts to be used and discarded, used and abandoned, used and never looked back at again."

I share the same view as Osho, when he writes: "My approach is: use the boat, use beautiful boats, use as many boats as possible, with this awareness, when the shore is reached the boat is abandoned with no clinging. While you are in the boat, enjoy it, be thankful for it. When you are out of the boat, say thank you and move on"[28].

---

[28] Quotes are from Osho's "*The Book of Wisdom: The Heart of Tibetan Buddhism. Commentaries on Atisha's Seven Points of Mind Training*"

"And what is this [working in recovery], *anyway,*
as a human activity or as a vocation,
or as a profession, or as a hack job,
or perhaps even as an art,
and why do so many people feel compelled to do it?"
[Margaret Atwood - On Writers and Writing]

In a way or another, we are all addicted: to what people think of us, to creating melodrama mistaking it for excitement, to our past, to anxiety and negative thoughts. There is nothing special about you, nothing so unique: we are all in the same boat. We are all breathing living beings with fears, pain, aches, hopes, and dreams. Let me tell you this: working in recovery, sometimes, is not altruism: it's co-dependency. You need to still be there to feel safe. Co-dependents are selfish and working in recovery is often a self-destructive behaviour. It doesn't do you any good. It is the desire for belonging and pseudo-innocence. And there is the risk of hurting others in the process.

Addiction is not found in recovery. Addiction is out there, in the streets, in your office, in your factory, down at the pub, in your family. Go there, help there, assist there.

Go out, breathe, walk your path. As they say: walk the talk; but you really have to walk it first! Explore, live. Then, if you are still interested in collaborating, go back. But only *after*. Altruism is courageous and contagious. Co-dependency is fearful. And very dangerous.

One common denominator in people in addiction, and of their family members, is the lack of trust. The very basic lesson in life: trust others and trust yourself. Trust means having clear boundaries, a strong sense of integrity, courage; it means being reliable and accountable. Brené Brown gives a detailed definition of trust, using the acronym B.R.A.V.I.N.G.: Trust as braving connections.

B.R.A.V.I.N.G. as boundaries, reliability, accountability, the Vault (confidentiality), integrity, being non-judgemental, and generosity. In the Appendix you will be able to find a more detailed description of same, including the link to the video.

Erikson of course puts trust at the very beginning of the lessons we need to learn. He also suggests that we, as adults, in order to regain and re-learn trust, should work on hope. Unfortunately, there is a very fine line between hope and faith. Having faith in a community which assists you, can be comforting. Finding faith can be extremely soothing. Substituting hope and trust with blind faith is, instead, dangerous. I have unfortunately witnessed many people in my life who felt lonely and lost, emotionally weak and very frail, and who uncritically joined groups, communities, and churches, where a subtle conditioning was masqueraded by faith. I can imagine that it can be pacifying for someone's soul to finally find the father they never felt they had. Feeling they belong somewhere, discovering their identity.

Please, do not stop enquiring.

When we limit ourselves with low expectations,
the growth of the tree of happiness ceases.
The power of growth, of improvement,
the power to overcome all stagnation
and break through every obstacle
and transform a barren wasteland into a verdant field
— that unstoppable power of hope
resides right within your own heart.
It wells up from the rich earth of your innermost being
when you face the future without doubt of fear:
"I can do more, I can grow.
I can become a bigger and better human being."
Life is a never-ending struggle to grow.

[Daisaku Ikeda]

potatoes

Start with You.

And now, for some hard truths:

1. You are nobody's circus. You are nobody's monkey.

2. Nothing has to happen for you to feel good.

3. You are the only person responsible for your own happiness.

4. You can be happy for no reasons whatsoever.

5. As long as you structure your life where happiness is dependent upon something or someone external, you will experience pain.

6. You set up the rules for your life; make them so that you can win.

7. Set your own Commandments:

    i. Be you
    ii. Let it go
    iii. Do it now
    iv. Enjoy the process
    v. Do what needs to be done
    vi. (etc)

8. Do not wait for another crisis to remake 'n' reshape your life.

9. Reading and knowing about 'meditation, mindfulness and awareness' do nothing.

10. What's important is what lies within you.

11. Authenticity is the most important potential: only you can be you.

12. Too many *shoulda, coulda, woulda*…

13. "You will get nowhere if you go about *what iffing* like that". (Roald Dahl)

14. You can turn poison into medicine.

15.Happiness happens with personal inner transformation.

16.First things first.

17....

18....

19....

20....

21....

Our dear Carl Rogers, the father of Person Centred Therapy, compared human beings to a bag of potatoes, hidden in a cellar. Still, no matter what, potatoes do sprout. You can hide them as much as you want, but they need to exhibit their full potential: they sprout, they want to become plants which make more potatoes. That's all they know, and that's all they will do, regardless of their conditions.

It is the same thing for human beings: no matter where you put them, they want to feel better, grow, and make more human beings. You can close them in a cellar, in the dark, beat them up, shout them horrible things, hurt them, ignore them and abuse them: people always want to feel better. Evolve, expand, develop, grow; and then make love and make more human beings (or enjoy when other people make more human beings).

The first sprouting is the most difficult: you have to break the skin, it takes courage and pain. Some people know automatically what is good for them, others know a bit less. But they all want to (let's use a technical term here) self-actualise. As much as an acorn only knows that it is an oak, I want to fulfil my own full potential and to feel no more pain. For some people that first sprouting is going to college, leave a controlling relationship, change country, jump on a boat across the Mediterranean, change faith, start eating again, stop drinking, read a book, enrol into a dance class, start running, accept an invitation. For others that first sprouting, that first uncontrollable desire not to feel any more pain is self-harming, is drinking, is using drugs, is stop eating, is stopping talking. For others, their desire for stopping the pain is so strong, that their choice is suicide.

We all want the same things.

Love, affection, no more pain, no more hurt.

At times, with clients, I wish they could have seen me in the midst of my despair, in that cubicle, or on that road.

I wish they could now see the world through my own eyes: how beautiful it is, how full of potential, how many possibilities are out there. There's plenty of everything for everybody. There is!

The money I would like to earn has already been printed, the person I would like to date is already born, the car I would like to drive has already been assembled, the house I would like to live in has already being built, or its material has already been made. If not the material, its building block, its elements. Everything is out there.

What is it that you want?

What is it that you need to do in order to get it?

Are you thinking in terms of "you" or in comparison with others (yes, but he… yes, but she… you don't understand, my life is… and x said to me… and y did this… they are lucky… my situation… my family…)?

I haven't heard it all before: I have *said* it all before.

It is all down to you: you can choose.

Sometimes it's harder, sometimes it takes longer.

But no one ever can take you away from the option to choose: whether to move, to leave, to change; even if only to change how you see things.

I'll tell you a little story: one day I went to work and something 'major' happened the previous night. What really happened is not important; what is important is that it was 'major'. I entered into my room and there they were: one was in tears, one was really angry, one was fuming!, one was pacing, one felt betrayed, one felt annoyed, one didn't feel anything, one wasn't bothered in the slightest, one was angry that we didn't get on with the work as per usual, one felt restless. Still, the event that happened the previous night was the same for all of them: all of them were present, saw and heard the same thing.

The reactions, though, were multiple.

> *For instance, hungry spirits perceive the Ganges River as fire,*
> *human beings perceive it as water, and heavenly beings perceive it as amrita.*
> *Though the water is the same,*
> *it appears differently according to one's karmic reward from the past.*[29]
> [Nichiren]

---

[29] WND-1, 486

You can change your point of view, you can decide to see things in a different way. There's no fucking tunnel! There is no other shore! What you call tunnel, is actually your life. It's the Now. What do you want to do about it? Can you see beauty even when it is not there?

Because it is *never* not there.

How you decide to see things determines what kind of a person you are and are going to be: what your values are, what you focus on.

You must be firmly resolved.

Do not begrudge your fief;

do not think of your wife and children.

And do not depend on others.

You must simply make up your mind.

Look at the world this year as a mirror.

The reason that you have survived until now

when so many have died

was so that you would meet with this affair.

This is where you will cross the Uji River.

[Nichiren Daishonin – 1,829]

meanie, weenie, genie

I have never been an alcoholic, nor have I used drugs. Whenever I went volunteering at the beginning of my profession, among people in recovery from addiction, I always felt very conscious and a bit annoyed that I was mistaken for an addict.

"So, what was your choice: alcohol, heroin?" And I was thinking: C'mon, really? Look at me! And then I was replying "No, actually, I was never... I mean, I am not... I mean, my parents *bla bla bla*".

This, until I had to admit that I was still addicted: to drama and emotions; and nicotine. I was embodying a walking victimhood: *oh, poor me! My parents... the alcohol... the neglect... the poverty...* Let's admit it: I never really suffered poverty! My parents never really locked me in a room, beat me up so much that I couldn't move. I thought that my life had been horrible, until, of course, I heard some of the stories from my clients.

This does not mean that I didn't suffer, nor that I didn't feel any pain, nor that I did not experience any neglect or abuse.

What I have learned, though, and so well along the way, was how to fit in what is called the Triangle of Drama, or as I prefer to call it: The Meanie – Weenie – Genie.

This is how it works: in order to be a proper full-on Weenie with the badge of honour, you must have a Meanie in your life: oh gosh, my parents, weren't they bad? They didn't listen to me, they drunk, they did not love me enough, they did not show me affection, they chose my school, my clothes, my University, and life at home was Hell!

Therefore, I did the only thing I knew and copied my parents: I cried, sulked (a lot), emotionally blackmailed them, from a tantrum to threatening suicide believe you me, is very easy: I needed to attract attention, I showed myself off, I lied, I cried, I did the whole rigmarole. Until the Knight in a Shiny Armour, and on a White Horse arrived. And after him, there was another knight, and then I looked for a king, and then a new job, a new house, a new car, new clothes, a new book, a new project... a new rescuer. A new country. Some new adventure.

Nevertheless, because I never really changed, all these new rescuers, these Genies, did not pacify my soul, nor quenched my inner-thirst. So, I felt let down, again (and again, and again, and again) and all my rescuers turned into slaves I couldn't control and then into other Meanies. Round and Round we go...

Yes, I was addicted: to the Triangle of Drama. Part of me believes that when at the age of around two we get to know shame, control and labelling, that's when we all shape our own personal triangle and we step right in it, and then we spend most of our lives looking for someone whose triangle matches ours.

Being in that triangle is playing games, with self and others. My game was titled "I want you to do whatever I want you to do. And when I decide to test you, I will pack my bags and leave. At that point, I want you to run after me, chase me, and make me feel that I am important". No one run after me, ever. I left, slammed doors, tested, cried, got angry; literally I packed my belongings in an hour, once, and left. And when it didn't work, I changed player and tried again. Last time I tried that game, I have been actually thanked because I was leaving. Go figure! Call it backfire…

Getting out of that triangle is one of the most difficult things ever: it means being in charge. Of everything. Not just of the good things, but also, (or: especially) of the bad things. It means creating while being vulnerable.

The role of the Weenie will be swapped by the role of the *Creator*, with no expectations from others[30]. The role of the Meanie will, in turn, become the role of the *Challenger*: what can I learn from you, about me? I will not accuse you anymore, I will not blame you for anything, I will not get angry at you. Instead, my aim is to understand. And if I don't like what I hear from you, I know that I cannot change you. So, either I accept you as you are, or I leave. I know that the process of me changing cannot be stopped, and I do not want it to stop.

Therefore, instead of waiting for a rescuer, that will help me and support me and that I can then manipulate and control, I will look for a *Coach*, a Mentor, someone who will support me, and whose interest is my growth; and this is reciprocal.

All of the above cannot happen unless I change, first. Change starts with me.

---

[30] There is more and more on this here http://powerofted.com/

fucking spineless

It was an amazing sunny Saturday when I went to a daily course on self-reflective journalling. One of the exercises we did, was to write a letter about something that really bothered us. I don't know how it happened, but because of the type of work I was doing in the rehab at the time, I decided to try and write a letter to Mrs Nicotine, since at the time I was still smoking.

I got my pad out, my pen, and I started writing. Again, I don't know the reason why, but instead of writing the letter to my drug of choice, nicotine wrote to me. Her words were very clear, and it went something like that: *Dear Matilde, it is pointless for you to do this exercise and wanting to quit smoking because you are fucking spineless and I will see you outside in 5.*

Wow!

I was left breathless. It was so abusive, so controlling.

Was I really that spineless? Was I really so weak? How could I go, the day after, to work, teach and preach into a rehab, and then during midmorning break go outside, happily all together, to have a fag? Where was my integrity? Where was the boundary between an acceptable drug, sold openly in a shop, and a dirty, hidden and petty one? I was explaining how the brain works, and magic of the subconscious and the hidden mysteries of the unconscious and there I was, puffing away like it there was no tomorrow. And I knew, really, nothing.

My parents were alcoholics and co-dependent, and smokers. I was definitely co-dependent, and a smoker. Something needed to change.

What I did was that I took all the knowledge I had, all the plans I made, all the lessons I was teaching, and put them all to the test.

It went something like this:

During the month of September, I prepared myself. I still smoked, I did not reduce the number of daily cigarettes, which is highly counterproductive and stressful. I just noticed how I felt, and I journal about it. I noticed when I smoked, I noticed how I felt, I noticed patterns. And I wrote about it.

Then, I went to the local chemist and I asked to be enrolled in their 12-week quitting programme. They gave me literature, pamphlets, brochures, handouts. I consciously banned the cockiness of "I am actually working in addiction, I know…" and took them all, and read them all. And I journalled about it.

I decided that stopping for the month of October (which in the UK is synonym with the Stoptober programme for quitting smoking) was the best option I had. I asked the chemist to provide me only with patches. The reason being that I wanted to observe my mind at work: any cravings I would have had, were not due to a physical need (that was taken care of by the patch) but was only emotional and psychological, and possibly spiritual.

I decided especially not to use any lozenges, pastilles and especially e-cigs since, let's be honest, it is still "smoking": anytime you feel the urge and need, you stuff something in your mouth. At the root, nothing has actually changed.

I also decided to create something very personal, which was sewing a pouch where all my material and literature for the month of October would be stored. It felt an external manifestation of a personal desire and journey I was embarking on.

Then, I waited for October. I was actually ready and very eager to start a week before, but I think that part of my success was because I waited that extra week, I smoked those extra 175 cigarettes (if not more). Please, bear in mind that I quit before, and for about 4 years. Then, one simple phone-call and argument with my mother led me to grab one cigarette and then smoking a whole packet. Oh, I blamed her so much! It was her fault, it was her lifestyle, she didn't understand me, she hated me, I didn't feel loved, why did I have to have such a mother? Why was nobody helping me? *bla bla bla…*

The first of October arrived, and I started following the procedure: not smoking, cleaning the house, washing my clothes, reading, adjusting my diet, drinking plenty of fresh water, walking and journalling a lot.

What I noticed was that I didn't have physical cravings (thanks patches!) but gosh I *needed* that fag! I needed that fag that was replacing my courage in asking for time for myself: when I did not want to deal with certain people, when I did not want to engage with someone, when I wanted time for just me, when I wanted silence, when I didn't want to argue, when I needed a break: "I am just going out for a fag!" I could hear my voice saying. Now, I didn't have an excuse anymore. Not one. Now I had to find that courage and my voice to say: I am going, I am moving, I am nipping out for a sec, I do not want to talk, I need time and space for myself, I do not want to see anyone tonight, I want to do some outside thinking by myself, I am going for a wander alone, I do not want your company, I don't actually like you very much.

Gosh, that was my fag. It wasn't paper and tobacco, it was a whole armour and shield. Quitting smoking wasn't just finding some more breath, it was discovering a voice.

Something else I discovered was that I have often said to myself: Oh, I have washed the pots, now I can sit and have a cigarette; I have hoover/ironed/cleaned/read/wrote… now I can sit and have a cigarette! Well, I can sit, take a break, praise myself anytime I want, without having to smoke a cigarette.

I can enjoy myself without having to drink myself stupid. I can find the courage to leave my partner without having to use drugs. I can decide to change my job without having to gamble. I can decide my own happiness without having to overspend.

I can choose.

Every morning I was sitting on my sofa, in the living-room, with a cup of coffee in one hand, and my pen and journal in the other. I never actually had a proper craving. I was following the advice of the chemist, I was reducing the patches, I was still putting in the hours in educating myself with regards to my addiction. And my work was thriving.

And then, one Sunday morning, I was sitting on my sofa, in the living-room, with a coffee in one hand, and pen and journal in the other and I heard a voice. It was a strange voice: it wasn't from within, it wasn't from without. I was somewhere very close to me. It was towering and imposing, but somehow subtle at the same time. It simply told me: *Have a fag.*

Where was that voice coming from? Whose voice was it?

And then it dawned on me: I decided to do Stoptober and that day was Sunday the first of November.

There was a mocking and arrogant part of my brain which allowed me "to play with this quitting thing" while keeping track of the days. A part of my brain which I can only describe as having a life of its own. It was the scared part of me, the clingy one, the weenie; my default reset button, the "I know best", the "the old ways were the best", the "we don't like change, anyway!". The very cocky one. It was the almighty puppeteer.

It is my chimp. Do I want to let this chimp driving my whole life?

The conscious part of my brain, my state of awareness, was the one *telling* me what to do, and how to do it. It is still now that part that *says* who I am and *says* what I am going to do. It is the planner, the organiser, the one making lists. Then, my subconscious and unconscious, the hidden parts of my being, are who I *really* am, what I *really* do. I might want to wake up tomorrow morning at 4.30 am and look at the sunrise and then meditate, so the conscious me sets the alarm and prepares the clothes. The subconscious and the unconscious are the ones pressing the snooze button. Mind over mattress.

If we want real change, we need to make the sub- and unconscious work for us and the only way, in my opinion, is to understand what is it that we really want and like. That is where our deep-rooted values, and our integrity and congruence, can be found.

I might decide that I want to write this book: so, Ms Conscious Me sets the alarm for tomorrow morning at 6 am when all is quiet. She prepares the Moka for the morning and the favourite cup, cleans the desk, fills the printer with fresh paper, the desk is in front of the window overlooking the ocean. The room is pale grey and white… I mean, we all probably watched Diane Keaton playing the writer in "As Good As It Gets". I am motivated, I know why I want to write this book: I have some good ideas, and I have always loved writing. I think that this book is important. I have done my work, I have watched videos and listened to podcasts about the craft and art of writing. I *know!*

Next day, I wake up at 6 am, turn around, and go back to sleep till 8 am. I do not write a word. Not one single word during the whole day. The mojo is gone. Diane Keaton turns into a snotty critic who constantly reminds me that I will never be able to achieve anything in life. And, if I were still smoking, that is what I would do for the rest of the day.

But if I imagine myself with this book published, and maybe someone sends me an email saying that they found it helpful, I would feel particularly pleased with myself; and then, maybe, someone invites me to talk about Buddhism and psychotherapy, and in order to do that I happily drive to this venue, while listening to good music, and stopping at a quaint restaurant to eat some grilled fish; and at the venue I meet some incredible people with whom I spend some amazing enriching time exchanging experiences and opinions… you bet that I am at that desk writing at 6!

I listen to my sub- and unconscious, what we really want, what makes us truly happy. I give my monkey a banana, or better, some grilled fish on a day out while interacting with interesting people.

And here is the book.

I didn't quit smoking because I wanted a better health, more money, not to stink of tobacco, and to please my cat. Those are by-products. Every person experiences the same thing: nothing unique to me[31]. Every person who quits smoking will have a better health, will cough less, will have more breath, and more money in the pocket. And their kids, partners, friends, parents, cats/dogs will feel happier.

They are not the reason, though.

My reason was Freedom. The main core value of my life is Freedom. I can't smoke and feel free at the same time.

I can't tell you that you *have to do* something, without going against my own core value.

I can't tell you that my theory is the best, because I would overstep your freedom.

I can only be an eclectic therapist because I cherish freedom.

---

[31] Please, watch Simon Sinek's TEDtalk on *Start with Why*. You will thank me later. You can find it here: https://youtu.be/u4ZoJKF_VuA

I do not like emotional ghettos, nor labelling, because of freedom.

"We don't realize that,
somewhere within us all,
there does exist a supreme self who is eternally at peace."
[Elizabeth Gilbert]

I know I tapped into that sacred and eternal part of me, the observer of my thoughts, my "awakened mind", as described by Dzogchen Ponlop. My Rebel Buddha. I found that everlasting and pure part of me who never needed nicotine, who never smoked and was never addicted.

And who has always been free.

We can definitely change any situation or environment
by transforming our fundamental mindset
and revealing our Buddha nature.
All fear vanishes
the moment we fully believe that
"I alone write the script for the drama of my life."
[Daisaku Ikeda]

no

Start Now.

Start by recognising that if you change, things will change, and the people around you will have to change: either they go through their inner transformation, or you will change tribe. Be aware of one important rule: no one can make you change. In the same way: you cannot change anyone. Change has to be personal, in order to last. If someone decides that they are going to change because of you, it will not last and they will turn into frustrated and resentful beings. Would you like to have the whole responsibility for someone else's happiness? Then, don't ask for anyone to carry yours.

If you want to change, you have to do it for yourself and yourself only: not your children, your spouse, your family, your Country, your Church. You, and you alone. I have met too many at times people who decide to quit smoking (very simple example) for their children. When cravings arrive, they internalise the blame for the kids for not being able to smoke, and then if they can't smoke, they feel awful; and they want to smoke *because* they feel awful and unhappy, deeply unsatisfied. They made a promise, though, to those little kids who in the evening they will hug, smelling all fresh, while feeling resentful, unhappy, and filled with cravings from head to toe. There is no change, then. You have simply taken away the substance. Nothing has really changed.

I have often seen people going out of rehab centres and back into their families, for them to go straight back to their substance of choice, because the family did not want to change, did not want to adapt and get to know this new person. They come to me and tell me that they don't understand: they quit, they stopped, they changed, they took the right steps, they made amends, they asked for forgiveness, they did what needed to be done and still: they are not understood, they are not accepted. I saw wives not wanting their husbands to stop drinking because being the "wife an alcoholic that everybody can pity and support" is the only role they knew. "Look at me, I'm such a good woman, I tolerate day after day, as the Holiest of Holy, what is going on: him drinking, him spending the money, him no working; I raised the kids, by myself; I did all of this, by myself, how good am I?"

Well, no, you are not.

Because you don't understand nor accept change. And you are scared. And you play the blaming game.

If your husband changes, your dad changes, your mother changes, well you have to be ready to change, grow, and stop blaming. Too many a times I felt, as a daughter, way more comfortable when my parents were drinking: no one was checking on me, no one to tell what I had to do, where I had to go, who I could talk to; I had a perfect excuse: they were drinking! And look at me: how sad was my life? Wouldn't you help someone like me, with 2 alcoholic parents? Wouldn't you rescue me, do things for me, excuse me, tolerate me?

Well, it doesn't work like this, in real life and among adults.

If you want to change, you have to accept that people will not like it, and they will try to stop you, they will try to make you feel guilty, they will find excuses for you not to go to college, university, change job, change career, change partner; they will tell you haven't got enough money to start a new life, and that they have suffered enough because of you and now it is *their turn*.

You will find people who will tell you that going back to college, change your life, move abroad can't be done, that especially *you* can't do it, that 'there's nothing you can do" to change the situation, that they know best.

They will get envious, angry, frustrated, hurt; you will wonder what you have done so wrong to deserve all of this: well, let me tell you: nothing, simply changed, simply decided to be you. They will treat you with disdain, disregard; they will try and belittle you and ask you who the hell you think you are!

They will know best, what is right for you: they are the fortune tellers, the mind-readers. They will show you how ridiculous your ideas are, they will plead for you not to try anything new, because otherwise you will get hurt, and they told you so, and they have your best interest at heart.

And then, they will get sick: emotionally sick, physically sick.

I heard them all. They keep on coming, even now: why do you have to sit there and write while you could go and find a job? Why don't you come back home (*to look after me*)? You are way too old to start again!

It is called: control.

Remember: they are not you. Unfortunately, whatever they think, and believe, and they say around about you, it not your business. If you stop and listen, you have been side-tracked; and they have won. You could decide to stop and argue, complain, ridicule, spread rumours about them, threaten them as much as you feel threatened, or emotionally blackmail them as much as you feel blackmailed. Don't forget that in order to do all of that, you have to stop on your journey. Is it worth it?

Don't stop. There is a saying: you can play with the pig, but only one of you will enjoy it; and it's not you, in the long run. Defending, justifying, explaining: it is not worth it. You have your life to live, they have theirs.

Do not retaliate, do not use sarcasm, do not fight back: I know that we all want to be liked and accepted; and by stopping and explaining, our main aim is always to be understood, accepted and that they would change their minds and come back to tell us that, you know what? we were right!

It doesn't work like this. We can't change them, and we are not interested in explaining. We are more interested in our journey, in our direction, in what we are doing with our own lives.

I had a couple of clients who nicknamed me "the breakdown therapist" because it seemed that many of the ones who went through recovery, when out of the rehab and back home, broke up with their partners. First of all, whatever clients do is not my business and I am not responsible for their choices, whether they break up or use again. True is, though, that if you have met your partner while in addiction (and I use the term *addiction* in its broadest sense), the moment you stop using, and start changing, and go "back home", you might realise that this person is not for you. Not anymore. Not for this stretch of the journey. The penny drops, especially if this person is still in addiction, still displaying compulsive attitudes, still in full triangle of drama, still co-dependent.

You have changed. They have to change to.

There is only one legitimate authority, in your life: and that is you. Only you. No one else. You have to decide if you want happiness, if you choose happiness, if you deserve happiness, if you want to experience happiness. You have to decide if you want to change.

There is, hidden somewhere in there, something we call Real Self: you at your purest form, your desires, your dreams, your Buddha status, the Holiest Part of Self, what you always wanted to do, those thoughts you seem to go back to over and over again, those subjects you always talk about, those people you meet and who remind you, even at the age of 50, that you really wanted to take up surf and move to California when you were 10. Or maybe, you had this dream of becoming an astronaut, a brain surgeon, a dancer, a mother, to raise sheep somewhere in the North of Wales.

Then, within you, there is this other part, the Conditioned Self, or Idealised Self, moulded and conditioned and idealised by others: oh, an astronaut, don't be silly! A brain surgeon? You need to go to work, stop thinking about college and university (we don't have any money; you have to look after me; well, you got pregnant!). Most of the time we live following our Conditioned Self: it seems to be the only thing we know, about us. Then our Real Self shows up: at Christmas, when we see others *oh so happy* and we are given the same boring present; or at Valentine's when we see others *oh so happy* and you don't feel in love or loved anymore; or at Birthdays when we should feel *oh so happy* and we are reminded that times flies and another year is gone, and nothing has changed. We feel pain. We feel sadness. We feel a void at the top of our stomach, a sense of hunger and urgency. Fear.

We could get frustrated, angry; or we swallow pain and emotions and develop gastritis; we storm out of houses slamming doors; we "fall in love" with the wrong person and for all the wrong reasons; we can't sleep, we can't eat, we lose or gain weight, we drink too much; or we start using recreational (or not so recreational) drugs.

There is a fight, inside, that has been going on for years.

And you can't shut the Real Self up: never.

Let me tell you now: it will never shut up. Because it is you.

Clients come to me because they drink too much, or they can't sleep, or they have been suffering from anxiety. They might have punched someone, or they walked out of (another) job, they had a panic attack, they fell in love with someone at work and they can't understand what is going on. Part of them is also very bitter: they never smile, they have given up. They are turning into grey puppets in the hands of others.

There is a fight, that's what is going on. Their Real Self wants to be acknowledged, and the more they try to shut it, the more he screams, shouts and has a bigger tantrum. Their Real Self wants to express itself, wants to have its voice heard, wants them to have courage and say that they are really sorry, but there is only one life, and they hope to be understood; but as much as they are aware that it all might sound really silly, they are going to enrol in a dance class, because (you know what?) they always wanted to dance[32].

You know you are way too old to become an astronaut, but there is a local group of *aficionados* who spend hours watching the Moon at night and you are going to join them, now. Because tomorrow is too late.

The only thing we have is *now*. The past is gone, and future does not yet exist (if ever). There's only now. And this very moment is the most precious thing. You can choose what to feel, and how to behave, and how to respond.

You can choose what to do.

You can decide that it is too late, for you; and that it is too hard, too difficult, too complicated. And you are too tired. I am ok with that.

Or you can decide that you can give it a try, and you can teach your children what it means to be really adventurous in Life, by being responsible for your own happiness. It takes one decision, and then one day, and another day, followed by another day. And a whole sequence of days.

That's all it takes.

---

[32] Fancy watching "Shall we Dance?" with Richard Gere and Jennifer Lopez?

[ps: do you know why you meet always the same type of jerks? Why all of your bosses are horrible? Why your relationships last always 2 years tops? Why you end up rejected? Why you are always broke?]

There must have been a time in which you learned what it meant to survive, how to be safe. You learned it and made it yours. Was it a day you saw something painful and then went out with your friends and saw them getting drunk and you thought: this is better than what I just experienced? Or was it a series of shameful events, of put-downs, of pain and you went out with your family and they drunk and laughed, and you thought: well, that's better! Or was it constant neglect, and one day you might have entered a Church, a cult, a group, a meeting; you felt safe there because people there seemed to "get it", so you kept on going back every day because that meant safety for you?

When did you learn how to survive? What did you learn? What does survival mean to you?

With strength and passion

Anything is possible—

Even stone tigers

Must fall before an archer

Whose conviction is complete.

[K.9 – Gen. Stone Tiger]

the buddha's invitation

By David Hare

Will you come to eternity's tentative edge
then teach the world of its unspoken power?
Will you plunge filthy waters with only your faith
then fly to the heavens on hope's thinnest breath?

Will you squeeze yourself through to the middle of you
yet still keep a space for those who might hate you?
Will you sit with the scream at the core of your soul
and then share your song with those who might love you?

Will you dive, will you run
Will you rise with the sun
Will you laugh, will you weep
Will you chant till you sleep?

Will you fashion your future from garbage and grit
yet keep one hand free for those who would hold you?
Will you bet all you have on an unfancied truth,
then share your raw wisdom with those once were brave?

Will you cast off your shackles, your comforts, your props,
Will you scrap sweet illusions for a Law that could break you?
Will you trade your bravado for slivers of faith

Will you silence your mind just to follow your soul?

Will you give up your status, your perks and your pride,
Will you join me in exile, where many have died?
Will you strip bare the critic, the cynic, the fool,
All the roles you have played, all the clichés, the rules?

Will you sit with the tramp, and the thief and the whore,
Will you keep giving hope when they ask you for more?

And if I stand by your side on this grand Treasure Tower
Will you smile, will you shine
Will you say what you saw?

Will you dance, will you chant,
Will you promise me more?

Will you risk, will you write
Will you make a new Vow?

Will you stand, will you fight
Will you come with me now?

a believer

Start with searching.

I remember a warm day in October 1996. My dad passed away the previous year and his brother, for my birthday, gave me a copy of *The Celestine Prophecy* by James Redfield, telling me: "I don't know what to make of this. You just read it". Funny enough, we never actually spoke about the book, ever, after that.

For me, though, after what I went through and how lost I felt, everything seemed to make sense, after that day. I didn't just *read* the book: I lived it, felt it, experienced it.

The *me* feeling, feeling too much, my family drama, the energy that permeates and connects everybody and everything: that book opened a world a meditation, reading, more reading, more searching, less understanding, and at times feeling completely lost. You also have to remember that it was the end of the 90's in a very Catholic and hence somewhat closedminded Italy. All this New Age stuff was frowned upon. I wanted more, though; I searched, looked, wrote, experienced and felt more. It was painful and exhilarating and unfortunately very solitary. I have been hopping skipping and jumping between the Church and New Age for years, trying to make sense of it all. I bought Bibles and Apocrypha, dictionaries of Greek and Latin, read extensively and, again, felt very lost in the process.

I have to publicly admit that the only person who supported me in this process was my ex-husband: I "render to Caesar the things that are Caesar's". (Romans, 13:1)

After *The Celestine Prophecy* and its sequels, I moved to Dan Millman. At the time I decided that I wouldn't believe in anything anymore and supported by cynicism and arrogance, I enrolled in an online Science degree at the Open University. I decided that I would have looked for God's algorithm myself, trying to make sense of my own internal chaos. I studied Biology, Chemistry, Geology, Volcanology, Environmental Systems, Ecology, and fell in love with the Gaia Theory. Something, even from a scientific perspective, started making more sense in my life. I didn't know how to translate that into a job, so I kept on writing and taking pictures on the side.

I was confused, and eager, which can be a very dangerous mix.

I could sense that there was no definite end between the tip on my finger (where some cells decide that that's the end-point), the air around it, and then the object close to the finger. From a microscopical perspective to me, it was all a continuum. Macroscopically, I could feel it.

I met some Jehovah Witness and joined them for about three years. I felt that my Christian guilt was still very strong in me nevertheless pacified, but I could not accept what I can only describe as cultural narrowmindedness, the relentless explaining of their theories using their own books, this land of circular reasoning which sat so bad within me. "God knows what is best for us, and he is the source of all wisdom. By listening to him, you will become truly wise." (Proverbs 1:5). I felt that hearing that "God knew best what was right for me" when spoken in the voice of a human being from a pulpit, sounded too much like my mother. And I didn't like it. It was a painful goodbye because I knew that they were (and still are) very good people, with very good intentions, and a commendable (and enviable) strong belief. I have learned so much, from them. Still, to this day, I fondly remember some of their publications. But they were not for me. I know I found a second home, in there. I felt accepted, a sense of belonging I was missing at home, and an easy way to carve my own identity.

But it wasn't me. And it wasn't for me.

Merely belonging and identity are not what Faith should be about. "The purpose of faith is not to turn people into sheep; it is to make them wise. Wisdom isn't knowledge that causes suffering for others; it is enlightened insight for improving one's own life as well the lives of others"[33].

As you would, I dived straight into paganism: energy, tarot, looking for a missing link between my own land, and the land of old; connecting my dissertation on Beowulf, Christ, German Philology, moon cycles, and the field just behind my own house.

Lost, again.

---

[33] Ikeda, WISDOM, vol. 2, p. 33

My soul was crying out of desperation. That little girl who was painting little nuns in a row was lost. I did not feel the love of a family, did not feel the love of God the Father. At times, I was going back to Church but knew too much to sit there in silence. I felt I could stand up and shout: you are lying!

I had no real faith, only questions. And envied any person who did not ask questions, who was happy with whatever he found, even if it was nothing. My unsupported restlessness led me to look for love in all the wrong places, hurting many people.

My triangle of drama was strong within me.

On my path of discovery, I jumped from Christianity to Zen, dipping my toes into Taoism, New Age (again), astrology, Osho, Hinduism, strict Catholicism, and Wicca. I think I tried them all.

I was desperate for an answer. I was desperate for a sense of belonging and identity. I had no way to answer the question: who am I? Am I a woman, a wife, a daughter, a Christian? What about all the pain I had to endure in my life: was it all for nothing? What's the point of being here, in the World, now?

Little did I know that I was searching for the answers to the four classical existential questions: on the reliability of people, on the unknown that has to come and that I cannot control, on the concept of chance[34], and on death and endings.

---

[34] There is an entry, in my journal, that goes something like that: "what if being a survival twin, surviving an extremely difficult birth and not being fed for the first three days of my life; what if surviving an earthquake at the age of 8; what if all my surviving, all my searching and struggles led me here, now, to this very moment, just

I was longing at times for a spiritual lobotomy, something, *anything*, that would pacify my soul. Every time I was reading something new, I could grasp it intellectually, believed every word in it for the following couple of days and then vehemently criticise it and condemn it, because it wasn't working, it wasn't giving me any peace. My father's saying that God had "many passports" wasn't quenching my thirst.

I only had a couple of memories I was holding on tightly, and I do to this day: one night, I woke up and felt intensely that God existed; so much I had to wake up my husband to tell him; and then one day I was sitting on a chair, on a very hot summer day, in Udine, while I was reading *The Celestine Prophecy*, and an intense calm came over me or expanded within me and I felt at once me, part of me, part of a whole, and the whole being me, all at the same time. Everything started to glow, and I felt very light and at peace. If I close my eyes now I can still feel the same experience in my body.

What if, then, my panic attack was nothing more than a spiritual experience?

I now know that all these past years I have tried to make sense of two completely different experiences: in one there's an external almighty God the Father, white beard and all, all-encompassing and all-deciding; in the other one, I am daughter and God at the same time. My strict Catholic understanding, nor any *proper* Christian doctrine would

---

to understand that they meant *nothing*, that I am destined for nothing, that there is no Call, no Mission, that it is all just pure chance, it is only fortuitous, purely accidental. That there is no meaning nor code to crack. That I am ordinary. What if?"

have accepted the New Age experience; most of the New Age energy-based experience did not accept the concept of a God the Father. I was stuck in between, and very unhappily so. I tried in so many different ways to connect the two, to pacify and make those two sides of a coin to agree and approve of each other.

I joined the Church many times during these 20 years: whether Catholic, Anglican, Evangelic, Methodist and even one of these new modern ones with electric guitars and Holy Spirit descending on people in ecstasy (or on a bunch of women on the front row all infatuated with the pastor). I lasted a couple of months, if not less. Then I dived into Hinduism, and Tara and Tantra, chanting mantras and using mudras for another couple of months, feeling very guilty and getting nowhere. One of the questions I have always been asked was: why? Why do you need to know? My answer has always been: Imagine if I die, now. I go up there, somewhere, and I really meet God, and he tells me: *I told you, it was all written there, black on white. Why didn't you follow it?* I need to know. If that is the Truth, why don't I believe it?

I was petrified of making the wrong decision. I mean, we are talking eternity here, guys; not a week, or a month, or a lifetime. We are discussing *infinity*.

When I felt let down by any organised religion, and by God Himself, I turned to philosophy, loving the Stoics and listening to the soothing voice of Alain de Botton.

When psychotherapy entered my life, things got complicated for a while; but then everything started making much more sense: and I listened to Nicoletta.

Nicoletta is the kind of friend I would hope for all of you to find. She is compassionate, helpful, present. A good listener. A beautiful soul. Nicoletta did not have the opportunity that I had with regards to study. She didn't read all the books I read. Still, she is not stupid. She found the answers I was looking for, just with her heart.

I travelled, I moved, I read, I studied, I argued and searched. She felt. And chanted.

She told me about Nichiren, and Nichiren Buddhism. She didn't quote from books. She chanted. And I listened.

It is because of Nichiren Buddhism, that I am writing this book. It is because of Nichiren Buddhism that I understand now so much more and can connect my past with my future, through my present.

Buddha was a rebel. Nichiren was a rebel: "always stood free from the confines and constraints of existing religious convention or authority"[35]. The three presidents of the Soka Gakkai (which is the association of Nichiren Buddhists I belong to) were three rebels: Tsunesaburo Makiguchi died in prison because of his faith; Josei Toda decided to follow him to prison, because of his belief; and Daisaku Ikeda decided "to dedicate [his life] to *kosen-rufu* (i.e. to spread and declare Buddhism) with the spirit of a revolutionary ready to give his life for the cause if need be"[36]. My clients who want to leave their well-

---

[35] Ikeda, VICTORY, vol. 2, p.94
[36] Ikeda, VICTORY, vol. 2, p.7

established triangle of drama, pain, and addictions, are rebels. And I feel safe among rebels.

Buddha tells us that it is not important to know if God exists or not. It is not for us to know. Instead, he teaches me to look inside for the answers, to take full responsibility for my own happiness and my future. To be courageous. "Outwardly we might look like *Bodhisattva of Poverty* or *Bodhisattva Sickness*, - President Toda says - but that is merely a role we are playing in the drama of life"[37]. I am tired of my Triangle. Buddhism teaches me to make my voice heard because someone somewhere needs to hear what I have to say.

As Nichiren Buddhists, we believe in the Lotus Sutra as the only writing which reveals the true intention of the Buddha, which was to save all people[38]. The Lotus Sutra, or by its proper title of *The Sutra of the Lotus Flower of the Wonderful Dharma*, or *Myoho Renge Kyo*[39], has been described by one of its translators, Gene Reeves, as a *polemical document*, an *inspirational text*, but also *one of the greatest religious scriptures and most influential books*. A book that will change your life.

---

[37] Josei Toda in Ikeda, VICTORY, vol. 2, p.65

[38] Any further explanation and description is mainly taken from the Soka Gakkai Nichiren Buddhism Library online that you can find here : https://www.nichirenlibrary.org . Please, do bear in mind that I am trying to explain some Buddhist concepts in the easiest possible way. You can find more info in the Bibliography and Reference part of this book. Other references are as described.

[39] *Myoho*: Mystic Law, *Renge*: lotus flower, *Kyo*: sutra. Nichiren has added *Nam* to indicate 'devotion to'. As Nichiren Buddhists we chant *Nam Myoho Renge Kyo* as the invocation established by Nichiren on April 28th, 1253, which encompasses all laws and teachings included in the Lotus Sutra itself.

Shakyamuni Buddha tells us that all the previous teaching he has taught (that he describes as *three vehicles*) were only provisional; they were expedient means in accordance with people's different capacities at different times[40], and which were provided with the final aim to lead people to the only true status of supreme awakening as described and offered in the Lotus Sutra itself. Reeves even states that this *one vehicle* of the Lotus Sutra can be understood as *nothing but skilful means [...] a teaching device, a skilful means of teaching that the many means have a common purpose*. Alongside, the Sutra explains to us the True Aspect of All Phenomena[41], it lists innumerable benefits of practising the Sutra, it explains the working of karma and how to change it and teaches us the doctrine of True Cause and True Effect of the enlightenment of Shakyamuni Buddha. Most of all, it teaches us in a very subversive way (taking into consideration the times it was delivered), that we can all attain Buddhahood in this Life Time, exactly as we are, with all our faults and quirkiness, pains and miseries, pasts and short-comings. It is only the Lotus Sutra that "teaches the attainment of Buddhahood by women"[42] and that "a woman who embraces this sutra not only excels all other women, but also surpasses all men"[43].

---

[40] "[It] takes into account the spiritual condition of the people, the state of society and of the country, the teachings and beliefs that prevail there, and so on." Ikeda, VICTORY, vol. 2, p.27

[41] The True Aspect is the True Reality of Everything, that nothing is really separated, that we are all made by the same substance and carry the same potentiality.

[42] WND-1, 931

[43] WND-1, 464

Enlightenment in the Sutra is grounded in the doctrines of "mutual possession of the ten worlds" and "three thousand realms in a single moment of life". The whole Universe is embedded in what we would call the Mystic Law, the truth and principle of Life, the Essence of what we are. As human beings, we are subject to constant change and transformation since life is never fixed. This happens while we move from one life-state (or condition) to another. Nichiren Buddhism describes ten specific life states, or Worlds, and divides them into four lower worlds: hell, hunger, animality[44], *asuras* (or anger); and into six higher ones: tranquillity, rapture, learning, realization, bodhisattvas, and finally Buddhahood (which is the state of perfect and absolute freedom in which anyone can realise the True Aspect of All Phenomena and recognise a Buddha in everyone, the life force which illuminates the positive aspects of each of the other nine worlds[45]). We all constantly change and hence we move from one life state to another: from one mood to another. We all change, all the times. Nichiren Buddhism teaches us that by being aware of which world I am in, I can decide to change because I can see my situation for what really is: I am free to transform. I am free to choose a different world.

Each World in itself has some positive and negative aspects: for example the world of Anger (the first one where Ego is revealed) can be seen as rage, egoism, self-righteousness, arrogance, conceit,

---

[44] These first three Worlds are also described as the three evil paths. Interesting to notice is that they do not contain the concept of Ego. In Hell, Hunger, and Animality there is no "I".

[45] I am providing a more detailed explanation of the Ten World as described by the SGI, in the Appendix.

dominion, and fear; I can decide, though, to use my status of Anger as passion to fight injustice, to create a better world, and a creative force for change. I can use my world of Hell not only to lift myself up, but also understand others, as a very powerful motivation to take action; Hunger as a yearning to improve myself and my community, Animality to protect and nurture Life. I can use the lessons learned when I was down, depressed, abused, hurt and rejected (my personal mud) and use them to grow and bloom as a lotus flower. I can turn my poison into medicine. We "can transform any kind of problem or suffering into fuel for our happiness"[46]. And since all the worlds are connected to each other, I can go straight from Hell to Buddhahood. Each world is connected and contained (not only as a potentiality) into any other one. Because of this, the Lotus Sutra is considered a Great Physician, because it allows me to attain Buddhahood as I am, straight from my pain, while still in pain. When I am hurt, rejected, depressed, suicidal, in prison; when I am in recovery, in addiction, even while using or when hurting others: I am already a Buddha. Every time we see someone in pain, or someone who is happy and smiling, or someone who has hurt us: they are all already Buddhas. And because we are also human beings, we will still make mistakes. We are imperfectly perfect Buddhas. Our pure Essence, or Soul, of Holy Spirit, or Buddha nature is within us at all times. Sometimes it is covered in dust and cobwebs and mud and dirt, and junk. By the act of chanting *Nam Myoho Renge Kyo*, our

[46] Ikeda, HAPPINESS, p.99

dedication to the Sutra itself, we remind ourselves where we come from and where we are going; of our Mission as Votaries of the Lotus Sutra; that we can change. Every moment is a good moment; every instant is a good instant; because the whole phenomenal world is contained within every single moment in life.

Personally, I never understood why I had to suffer so much in my life. What did I do so wrong that I had to cry so many tears? Why was I born in that family? I didn't have an answer that was satisfying until I met Nichiren Buddhism and its principle of Voluntarily Assuming Appropriate Karma. This can be found in the 10th Chapter of the Lotus Sutra, titled the *Teacher of the Law.* "It presents the picture of great Bodhisattvas who have accumulated immense good fortune and benefit and because of the benefit they have accumulated from their Buddhist practice, they could by rights be born in a 'good land'. However, due to their wish to save those who are suffering, they voluntarily create the negative karma to be born in such a realm and undergo the trials and tribulations of an evil age so that they can spread Buddhism"[47].

Tsunesaburo Makiguchi, the founding President of the Soka Gakkai, once said:

> To live one's life based on the Mystic Law, is to change poison into medicine. As long as we live in society, there will be times when we encounter accidents or natural disasters or experience setbacks such as business failures. Such painful and unfortunate events could be described as poison, or karmic retribution. But no matter what situation we face, if we base our life on faith, on the Mystic Law,

---

[47] As in https://www.hosshakukempon.com/iii-voluntarily-assuming-appropriate-karma-transforming-karma-into-mission.html

and exert ourselves in our Buddhist practice [...]
we can definitely turn poison into medicine
— transforming a negative situation into something positive.
VIC vol2 p. 61

Or natural disasters, he says.

"We should have the attitude: *These are sufferings I took on for the sake of my mission. I vowed to overcome these problems through faith.* When we understand this principle of 'voluntarily assuming appropriate karma', our frame of mind is transformed. What we have previously viewed as destiny, we come to see as a mission. There is absolutely no way we cannot overcome sufferings that are the result of a vow that we ourselves made"[48].

Let me tell you: this explanation is as good as any other. No one exactly knows what happened to us before our birth nor where our conscience and awareness are from, nor what will exactly happen to us when we die. To me, thinking that I might have chosen this life, that I might have consciously chosen my family in addiction instead of the Land of Eternally Tranquil Light, that I have chosen to remain a Bodhisattva instead of fully accepting enlightenment, that I have chosen to seek satisfaction in relieving the suffering of my parents and then others in order to lead them to absolute happiness (even if it

---

[48] Ikeda, WISDOM, vol. 2, p.208

costed my own enlightenment) makes some kind of sense; and I can accept my past pain and the choices I have made in my life.

I have been wondering ever since what kind of lessons I might have had to learn and then pass on. Maybe this is very simply my Mission: to accept my family past and history, understand forgiveness, and at the age of 50 write this book because maybe, someone out there, needs to read this.

The first vow of bodhisattvas is to save "innumerable living beings"; I start by saving myself. I will do this by understanding that when I am feeling down, miserable, anxious and rejected, I fall straight into a mixture of the world of Hell and the world of Anger. That is my default position, my auto-pilot, my habitual life tendency. My personal human revolution is to understand this, and then transform it. My auto-pilot is also my ignorance that we are all One and The Same, all belonging to the same Substance, Mystic Law, the Same Ultimate Truth. My laziness, apathy, and procrastination (let's call it with its proper name: fear of change) will try to stop me and hinder my change. That ignorance is called The Devil King of the Sixth Heaven: *He's my doubt, my poison, my karmic shadow. And He's all mine. No one else can claim Him. He is specific to me. When I make His voice King, I am one fucked monkey. In fact, He may be even talking to you right now: "Why are you reading this? Get off your ass and get a job, you worthless piece of shit. And stop eating those chips, you obese douche bag, you're getting orange grease on your PhD. Your friends are crap, your life is crap, you are crap." So that's Him. The Devil King of the Sixth Heaven. And just imagine what kind of action you'll take when His voice reigns — the lottery could make me a millionaire, my nose is too big, why can't I win an Oscar? Any Faustian bargain you care to make for money, youth, beauty, fame is the product of the Devil King of the Sixth Heaven. And He is so familiarly personal. He is part of you and me because we are human. In fact, He's at least 9 of the 7 Deadly Sins.*[49]

His voice is my mother's voice, my ex's voice, my teacher's voice, the pure animal fear, shame and embarrassment I experienced when I was a young girl, my childish reactions, my desires to be seen and noticed, my vulnerability. It is my hurt inner child, my chimp brain, my limbic system in over-drive. She is my Devil Queen of the Sixth Heaven. She needs to be happy, too.

Aren't the three poisons of greed, anger, and foolishness, the real causes of most of our problems? And what about attachment? I am reminded of the three of the four noble truths:

1. to live means to suffer: a life without suffering does not exist. Living in the pursuit of only one's happiness is Utopistic and unreachable. Using coping mechanism as escapism, such as alcohol, drugs, compulsive shopping, or any other form of "addiction" does not take the suffering away. It covers it, it masks it, but it does not erase it, remove it, or delete it.

---

[49] Adapted from https://wordpills.wordpress.com/2015/05/08/the-devil-king-of-the-sixth-heaven-explained-2/ : please, go and read the whole blog. You will thank me later.

2. the origin of suffering is attachment: it is our dependency on people, objects, status, the image of the Self; it is our fear of changing. It is focusing on what others think of us. Our clinging and holding on to a smokescreen of a life we are not really participating in; it is the attachment to the pain, the attachment to the cure, the attachment to the past, to our drama.

3. the cessation of suffering is attainable: just let go. Realise that you have never really owned anything, not anyone. You only belong to yourself. No one and nothing belongs to you. This will set you free. Happiness teaches Ikeda "rests on establishing a solid sense of self".[50]

Drop the comfort

Drop the drug

Drop the cure

Drop the boat: there is not even another shore.

While I keep on working on myself, while "buying bread and milk every day", I connect the dots between the experience I had that night of perceiving God, the day I felt I had no beginning and no end, that night I knew I was as old as the mountains; I can sort of understand how my mind works and where my thoughts are coming from, while seeing them from the perspective of my Soul, the Infinite Observer with No Origin and No End.

And for now, I feel joy.

---

[50] Ikeda, HAPPINESS, p.17

"If just being called a few names
or drawing a violent reaction
is enough to discourage you,
then you'd better off not bothering
in the first place."
[Josei Toda - Toda Josei Zenshu]

there is no end

Start with a choice.

And round and round we go: we began with a choice, we are getting close to the end of this book with a choice. It could be a different one or the same one. It still is a choice.

Your choice.

My choice was to sit here, at this desk, today, and write some more words.

This is how it worked for me.

As you know, I met the Buddhist practice via my Italian friend, Nicoletta. I received the Gohonzon[51] about 4 years ago in Lancashire and this is where I live and practice at the moment of writing.

About 2 years ago, hell broke loose again: a father figure I was very close to passed away, college ended, therapy ended, the job I had ended, a relationship I was in ended; I also experienced the painful end of a friendship, the death of a client, I had two particularly painful health scares and at the same some issues with the place where I live started. That was the end of me: I felt rejected from all fronts: personal, emotional, job-related. I felt there was no way I could make sense of

---

[51] The **Gohonzon** is our object of devotion, i.e. a scroll inscribed by Nichiren Daishonin with the Chinese characters "Nam-myoho-renge-kyo Nichiren" and representing our faith in its totality. This is contained in the **butsudan**, i.e. a shrine, or wooden cabinet that protects the icon.

why all of this happened in a very short space of time. I was also volunteering at Taplow Court (our main Buddhist centre) for a whole weekend, every two months, and I was looking for guidance and support. Almost at the same time, I started doing a course in Chaplaincy in Manchester together with one of my leaders, and my placement was together with a Catholic Deacon whose conversations and dedication re-ignited in me part of my dormant 41 years of devout Catholicism. I was feeling very confused and lost.

Leaders and fellow Bodhisattvas kept on repeating to me that I had to chant. That was the default answer I was getting. Unfortunately, it was with chanting I had a massive issue. I started with chanting with my eyes closed, and then chanting less and less until I simply stopped. I tried praying, but it didn't help either. I lost myself, and my faith, and friends, and a job, and college. I didn't know anymore who I was, I had no sense of identity. My days went by with me walking and crying for quite some time.

I was opening up to people, and I was getting the same stereotypical responses you would find on a glossy magazine. I felt like screaming: you are not listening to me!

You (person in front of me)

are NOT (really, I wish you could see and hear yourself)

listening (just fucking listen! And shut up!)

to me (me! Not someone else. Stop talking: this is not your agenda, darling; this is my stuff, concentrate on me!)

I felt un-acknowledged, un-heard, not-seen, rejected. Invisible. And I was surrounded by bare and dry land.

I felt that with what I was going through, I could connect more with my clients, the ones who never felt heard, understood, acknowledged. The rejected ones, the ones in excruciating pain, the ones with stories so brutal you would feel someone made them up.

I learned to stay, there. Simply to stay.

I needed someone to stay with me. I learned to stay, with them.

And I connected with Avalokiteshvara or Guanyin. She is an East Asian Bodhisattva associated with compassion and venerated by Mahayana Buddhists and followers of Chinese folk religions, also known as the "Goddess of Mercy". Some think that she is the precursor of the images we have of Mary, Mother of Jesus. She is also called the Bodhisattva Hearer of the Cries of the World and the whole of chapter 25 of the Lotus Sutra is dedicated to this figure: the Bodhisattva of compassion, empathy, listening, support. Wherever you need anything, or when you are in any emotional pain, in tears, frightened, abused, and rejected, call Avalokiteshvara and she will come, in multiple shapes and forms. The person who helps you in the street, that stranger who smiles at you, the friend who shows up when you most need him, the tax rebate when your wallet is empty, the sunshine when your car breaks down and you need to walk, your clients cancelling on you when you have decided you should really write and have no time, whatsoever.

I have learned from her, the Perceiver of the Cries of the World, to stay. I have also deepened my methodology, connecting to the three

195

pillars of Nichiren Buddhism: 1. Study (as in my philosophical approach), 2. Action (from Psychotherapy), and 3. Faith (my spirituality, and Buddhism): it is from the encounter of these three, that I operate. I understood then that I had to go back to basics: back to the Lotus Sutra, back to the writings of Nichiren Daishonin, back to Daisaku Ikeda and his guidance.

And you know how this works: the more you read and inquire, the more questions you have. Mine was mainly revolving around How: I was reading that I could express my Buddhahood in this lifetime, now: yes, but how? I can express my Buddhahood as I am now, I don't need to change: yes, but how? I can transform my pain, my problems, my poisons, into medicine and take care of my human revolution: yes, thank you, but how?

So, I turned into a very *Insecure Bodhisattva at the Frontline of a Human Revolution*, thinking I was really 'the worst person and therapist ever!

I went through phases when I felt powerless, apathetic, swamped, overwhelmed, burned out, very envious, angry, resentful, frustrated and extremely lonely (this is just to start with). I could picture myself as a radio, with aerial and batteries but no matter how much I turned the knob, I wasn't picking up anything. Not a thing. I was totally disconnected. Not receiving, nor transmitting. Life was going on somewhere else, not within me. I wasn't part of anything. That was me, just over a couple of years ago. And that *me* I didn't like at all, was still a

Buddha. Nichiren taught us that Life is a journey to the Truth that we ourselves are Buddhas[52].

I mean, guys, I am a psychotherapist, I knew what I was going through: transitions, menopause, endings, grieving, you name it: I could quote books and treaties and papers about my case.

While I was working in recovery at the time, finding myself in the mirror of the lives of my clients, I was using the concept of the 10 Worlds and how to turn poison into medicine. My question was, though, how can I see the magnificent Buddha Nature in my clients and in the people around me, including people who hurt me and don't respect my boundaries, if I could not see mine? Where is the compassion and understanding for myself? I was ready to stay with and listen to murderers and paedophiles, but not myself.

Daisaku Ikeda taught that only when we encounter problems we can understand faith: well, I wasn't understanding anything; hence, I was disappointing myself, again! I just wasn't getting it. And "not getting it" for me was tremendous, meant failing, meant getting old, giving up. I wasn't feeling. I was, again! into my own very personal and exclusive intellectual loop in which I do not let anyone in, where I can barricade myself, with books, looking for answers, always outside of me.

I could get, at times, a glimpse of something. I could feel like something summersaulting at the top of my stomach. Something was

---

[52] See http://www.sgi.org/about-us/president-ikedas-writings/the-wisdom-of-the-lotus-sutra.html

coming up: a tiny voice, which said, to me: chant. Sit there, and give it a try, again. What's the worst that can happen?

Every day I would come home, sit on my sofa, with dinner, cat, and remote and get a glimpse of my *butsudan*, open, inviting me to sit and chant. But, nope, I didn't. And I used to go to bed very guilty.

You see, I was teaching people to meditate, to sit and stay, to chant, to find themselves, to journal, to write. And within my own four walls, I wasn't chanting. Within me, something wasn't right.

One night something changed. One night I switched off the TV, still sitting on my sofa, and looked at the scroll, and it looking back at me. Why some people chant or pray, and others don't? I mean, we see it working, we hear of miracles, we read the stories, we listen to experiences. It works. Why don't we all do it?

What stopped me sitting there in front of the *Gohonzon*, and chant? I mean, it's about 2.4 meters, not more. Those were the longest 2.4 meters I had to cross. What was it?

I felt I couldn't move from my sofa, I could not go there and sit.

What stopped me from chanting where I was? I didn't actually have to move: I could have sat there, on my sofa, still holding on to my cat and my remote, and open my mouth. I so wanted to. But I couldn't.

Why?

And then it dawned on me: because all these chanting, praying and miracles work for you. They don't work for me. Because I don't deserve miracles, prayers, chanting, help, support. I felt not worthy and deserving to be neglected (which is the Mother of all Abuses). Even though my Mother was an alcoholic, a liar, an excessive, embarrassing, noisy, loud, fat, depressed, suicidal, and ridiculous woman, in my eyes I was worse than her. Because if I were a good girl, she would have loved me, and she would have stopped drinking. I was worse than an alcoholic, liar, excessive, embarrassing, noisy, loud, fat, depressed, suicidal, and ridiculous dead woman.

(pause to breathe)

If I were a Buddha, where was my self-esteem? So, I went straight back to therapy and realised how much, in my life, my default state was rejection and neglect, and victimhood. This was my karma, this kind of transparent sandwich board I kept on carrying with me wherever I went. Of course, you don't change years of default in a handful of sessions, but one thing was important for me: if I found my karma, if I found my auto-pilot, my habitual life tendency, if I found the default World I revert back to, I would have also found my Buddhahood! Because Buddhahood is contained in all the other Worlds. I had to go down there, where there is dirt, and pain, and puss, and foully smells, and horror, to find my shiny Buddha-nature. The moment I feel sad and melancholic, I don't like myself. But if I can see that person who is such a critic of the Self and love her just because she is a Human Being, I would automatically change my life state, and potentially experience Buddhahood.

I happily found my Inner Dictator, my own ignorance of my own worthiness, my fundamental darkness, whatever stopped me from chanting (and living) with my eyes wide open, and my head help up high. She was sitting in the dark, hugging my "jewel".[53]

At work I always say that we are here, in this World, to save people; to encourage people: this is our Mission. And it is very much ok if in this life we save only one person. It takes only one. And it is very much ok if that one person we save it is actually us. Because if we all saved ourselves, if we worked to transform us into the better version of us, the World would be such a better and lighter place to live in.

My Buddhahood is to transform my life over and over and over again. It will never be a race against time, because time does not exist, and there's no end. Ever. It is a constantly transforming, and adapting, and finding our own pace. I know I will be ok because I am a Buddha.

As much as you are.

Two years have passed.

Six months ago, again, I lost a job, a partner, another friend, another client, my car.

This time, I seem to have found myself. This time, instead of feeling like a half-empty old birthday balloon ready to get stuck somewhere and carried by the wind, I slammed back on earth. And felt everything, every single little thing. And it was painful.

And it was awesome.

---

[53] The "Jewel in the Poor Man's Robe" is one of the many parables in the Lotus Sutra and teaches us how we are unaware of all the treasures we possess within us.

Now I feel I am firm on the ground, not wobbly anymore, not disconnected anymore. Actually, I never felt as connected as I am now.

I don't exactly know where I am heading, what I am going to do next. If I stay, here, or I leave. If I will keep on working as a therapist, a chaplain, or a mentor as I am doing now.

I don't know.

But I have decided to be active, pro-active, instead of reacting.

I noticed I needed time, to feel the whole of the soles of my shoes firm on the ground. To understand where to go. To make my next move.

Emmy van Deurzen says that"transformation of our trauma in a creative way requires us to go beyond the wrongs done to us and not to oppose or avenge, but to transcend our pain and injustice"[54]. In order to do that, what we need is *commitment*, to take full responsibility in order to break free from a repeating cycle of crisis. I noticed that in my life I have never, consciously, made a commitment, be consciously dedicated to something. I realised only now that I entered into partnerships, jobs, living arrangements, most of the times because something else has happened before; I have always entered into something, preparing a way out, a door I leave slight ajar. For me. Because *you never know*.

---

[54] Emmy van Deurzen, QUEST, p. 123

This time I wanted it to be different. And as a proper girl would do, I got myself a takeaway and watched *Eat Pray Love* again because I needed a quote:

> *"I cannot find that feeling of devotion. -*
> *Devotion is love:*
> *pick somebody or something you want to be devoted to.*
> *This is about you. It doesn't even have to be God".*

Devotion can be defined as Love, Loyalty, Enthusiasm, Faithfulness, Fidelity, Constancy, Commitment, Dedication, Trueness, Adherence, Allegiance. Have I ever felt that way for anything? Or anyone? I don't think I have ever felt like that for *me*, never mind something else! It might have been subconscious, but never conscious.

I decided, with the support of fellow practitioners, to chant consistently for 90 days. My goal is, first and foremost, to prove to myself I can do it. I can commit, be dedicated and keep my word. When I quit smoking, that was a commitment for a month and then it has turned automatically into over two years, but when I started, I decided to do it only for a month. At the same time, I knew what worked for me, so I tackled this 90 days with the same approach: study, faith, action.

I have been reading and studying extensively.

I have chanted regularly every morning and every evening.

As for the action, well, you can imagine: this book came out.

I tried a couple of times before to sit and write 'my book', my 'therapy book', my 'book on addiction', I never went past the first draft of the introduction.

This time it felt different from the beginning, even if not easy. My fundamental darkness, my desire to stop, not write, take a day off, and avoid was huge. So great that I even started feeling cravings from cigarettes every time I sat at the laptop. I know what they are, where they come from, and they are not *me*: so, I give my brain a metaphorical banana, and I write some more words.

Change happens when you act, make that first step, decide.
When you choose.
When you choose that you want to change.
You know what they say: healing starts with awareness. There is nothing else you have to do, in the beginning, but being aware that there is something "not right" and that you want to change.

This whole process has also affected the way I work. I was discussing with my friend and colleague Samantha, the other day, on how only now I can define my practice which is supported by my personal 5 pillars:

1. Clients need to want to *change*, transform, go through their own metamorphosis. Whether they change as caterpillars (air), phoenixes (fire), salamanders (water), or snakes (earth) clients need to bring something to the sessions: I have to feel that there's something we can both work on. This can also be silence, and God only knows how many

203

silent sessions I had, but those are clients who keep on showing up, no matter what, who are not scared, who are sick and tired of being sick and tired; this resembles the Buddhist concept of going through our personal Human Revolution;

2. As much as I needed it when I was in pain, and what I experienced during my chaplaincy practice, I promise I will *stay* with the client. Stay to me means being non-judgemental, to empathise, to stay in silence, to cry or laugh, to attune to your needs. To stay. Part of me will somehow disappear, but it's just an illusion. I will stay.

3. I promise I will *not give up*, not on you, not on your story, not your past nor future. As long as you don't give up on yourself, I will not give up on you. This reminds me of *Siddharta*, by Herman Hesse, when he says that there are three things that he can do: he can pray, he can wait, and he can fast. I can wait.

4. My mission and aim are to encourage people to be *curious* about life: if you want to be my client or a member of my tribe, you have to be curious: about your journey, your path, I want you to read, explore, discover, be inquisitive, and then come back and teach me. Not having children, that is my legacy. I do detest (still in a compassionate and understanding Buddhist way), narrow-minded people, who wander around life aimlessly and wearing blinkers, never doubting anything, never asking any questions, and still never taking any responsibility and blaming everybody else. And it is so freeing to write this, now.

5. And finally, I do abide, even more so, to eclecticism and to being a *rebel*. If you want to experience Life by fully participating in your own Human Revolution, you need to be a rebel. Your revolution is only

yours and only you can dictate your own rules. Be a rebel, change them, morph, transform, alter, take a risk. Live.

One of the vows of Buddhism is to save every human being. Within those "every human being", there is me.

We come into this life to save people.
And it is ok if we save only one person.
And it is very much ok if this person you save is you.

This book has been written to save myself, for me to become a better version of me. It has been cathartic and liberating. This book is the book I was hoping to find 30 years ago: something which would have inspired me to move forward, not to give up; something I could carry with me always, that showed me compassion, understanding, and at the same time pushed me to be a better person and showed me a life outside of the Drama Triangle. Something that taught me that if you keep looking, you will certainly find. Something that nudged me into believing that there's always another option.

During these 90 days of chanting (which haven't finished yet at the time I am writing this) I have discovered also my personal reason for the daily practice: it is a way to check in with myself, to claim my own space, to define my boundaries, to make my voice heard, to find my congruence, to being comfortable in saying "no", to embrace my own vulnerability as part of my courage, to reveal my own truth, to remember to respect myself. It is howling to my pack.

It's finding my Tribe.

And to celebrate Me.

This just by chanting *Nam Myoho Renge Kyo*.

Of course, you might not find what you thought you were looking for, but that's the Beauty of it all.

We human beings have created our problems,
And I am confident we can solve them.
[...] we face a mountain of difficulties
— war and violence, oppression and poverty,
environmental destruction and so on.
We must make the twenty-first century an age in which
human beings resolve their problems
by first reforming themselves.
[Daisaku Ikeda]

one is the Mother of All

Nichiren writes that

> *if we inquire into the origin of Mount Sumeru,*
> *we find that it began with a single speck of dust;*
> *and likewise, the great ocean began with a single drop of dew.*
> *One added to one becomes two, two becomes three, and so on to make ten,*
> *a hundred, a thousand, ten thousand, a hundred thousand, or an asamkhya.*
> *Yet "one" is the mother of all.*[55]

Back in 1985, I was a student at *The United World College of the Atlantic*, in Wales. For two years I lived among students coming from 73 different countries: we learned about each other, about our culture, history, literature, politics. Heritage and Legacies. After those two years spent living among passionate like-minded students, I won a place to study English and International Politics in Scotland.

My mother and grandmother insisted instead that I went back home, to help, and to study Foreign Languages at the local University in Udine. In my grandmother's words "studying International Politics would bring additional bad luck to the family, since my mother's brother died when studying it in Milan". I left Llantwit Major at the end of May 1987 and managed to finally move back to the UK only in August 2008. And, as you probably remember, in August 1988 (almost a year after going back home), I lost consciousness and my memory. I lost me.

---

[55] WND-1, 667

The system of the United World Colleges[56], described as "a global education movement that makes education a force to unite people, nations and cultures for peace and a sustainable future" is founded on the words of Lester B. Pearson, who in his Nobel Lecture of 1957 said: *How can there be peace without people understanding each other, and how can this be if they don't know each other? How can there be cooperative coexistence, which is the only kind that means anything, if men are cut off from each other, if they are not allowed to learn more about each other?* Those words and that vision, which were engraved in our large hall in Llantwit Major, were still somewhere in me, even if dormant.

When I left college, in 1987, regardless of the dread of going back home, in that environment, I still hoped that I could do something, that I could in some way "change the world".

My life then changed abruptly (which seems a constant with me) and I had no cause to fight for, no battle, no desires, no commitment, no drive, no dedication. I envied people who were marching, protesting, writing, and singing Bob Dylan's or Fiona Apple's songs. I didn't have any of that. I didn't feel any desire to help any other human being. I was very much selfish and self-centred. Very much both egoistic and egotistic. I remember following the changes in China, South Africa, Germany, Yugoslavia, Iran and Iraq as if they were from another planet, and not touching me personally, even if I knew people who lived in those countries and who were at College with me.

---

[56] Please, see https://www.uwc.org/ if you would like to learn more about them.

Once back here in the UK and when I started chanting, I was fascinated by the ones who lived, marched, protested to the point of being arrested, because of their beliefs regarding fracking and the exploitation of natural resources. I still don't recycle as much as I could and I'm not fussy about plastic wrapping or where my meat comes from. I was living a very shallow life, in my own eyes.

Reeves writes when we think about peace is not "just for inner peace but for peace in families, communities, nations, and the world. Peace is not the mere absence of conflict. It brings joy and happiness to living beings and gives them the strength to share their joy and happiness with others, so that all can work together to transform the world into a pure land of peace". Would I ever find my battle for peace?

I did.

In a referendum on June 23rd, 2016, 51.9% of the participating UK electorate voted to leave the EU. Peace begins with respect, and boundaries and the UK decided to leave Europe.

Regardless of my occupation and the years I lived in the Country, I found myself feeling I had no rights, just overnight. I imagined that since it was 2016 and not 1930, no one would have ever forced me to leave, nor removed me from my own house. Still, I had many people questioning my right to stay; many people shared with me their fear "of the immigrants"; others confided to me that they voted to leave while at the same time found bizarre that I didn't have the right to vote. "Yes, but you are different" is the constant (and politically erroneous) response I get. Then others knocked at my door and asked me when I would leave, since this is not my Country. A couple of others shouted at me in the street. For these past two years I felt not wanted. I have been verbally abused. I felt I had no Country. I was very much feeling Ms Nobody.

But I found something to fight for: dignity. Not only my dignity, but the dignity of every human being, with their rights to live and to be treated fairly and with respect. I am not questioning here the validity of the referendum nor of its implementation: that is for the Country to decide. I am here considering the dignity that comes from ""firmly believing in one's own Buddha nature and that of others and therefore *respecting* all people".[57] Peace to me now signifies "refusing to condone violence or oppression that threatens human dignity or equality"[58]. My mission now, together with sharing my experience and Nichiren Buddhism, is "to forge a solidarity of peace and humanism throughout the world"[59].

President Daisaku Ikeda has met with the likes of Arnold J. Toynbee, Andre Malraux, Alexei Kosygin, Henry Kissinger, Kurt Waldheim, Nelson Mandela, Zhou Enlai, Rosa Parks, and Teresa Watanabe. Moreover, he met with the philosopher Richard von Coudenhove-Kalegi who was an early pioneer of the European Union. Ikeda was also one of the original supporters of the *Earth*

---

[57] Ikeda, VICTORY, p.30
[58] Ikeda, VICTORY, p.30
[59] Ikeda, VICTORY, p.38

Charter Initiative, which is co-founded by Mikhail Gorbachev, and he has included details of this Charter in many of his annual peace proposals since 1997. This year's proposal published in January, is titled "Towards an Era of Human Rights: Building a People's Movement"[60]. He writes: "One of the things we need to highlight is the need for migrants, like everybody else, to have their fundamental human rights respected and protected without discrimination on the basis of their status.". We can imagine how this applies to refugees and migrants. At the same time, it confirms the basis of respect for the dignity and fundamental rights of all the people, regardless of their status. I believe that the UK should now publicly guarantee the respect for the dignity of every human being on its territory, and that their economic, social, and cultural rights will be protected.

At the same time, and this is something that I feel very strongly, the UK should create (or at least allow) an educational program in schools which promotes international understanding and recognition of the importance of cultural differences and how much these do enrich a country. The UK should openly ban any form of racial, social and cultural isolation.

Hence, the scope of my new-found activism is larger than Brexit: is stems from *Bodhisattva Perceiver of the Cries of the World* and *Bodhisattva Never Disparaging*: Justice, Respect and Dignity will prevail. These "are

---

[60] Please see http://www.sgi.org/about-us/president-ikedas-proposals/peace-proposal-2018/index.html

not granted to us by laws or treaties; the imperative to protect the freedom and dignity of all people arises from the fact that each of us is inherently precious and irreplaceable". There is a need, more than ever, to address the "issues concerning international borders - strengthening immigration control in response to the influx of refugees and migrants, and territorial disputes over resources - [issues which] have gained prominent attention". Ikeda adds: "Throughout the world, we see disturbing examples of xenophobia in which individuals or groups are singled out as the objects of loathing, avoidance and isolation. [...] The New York Declaration for Refugees and Migrants adopted at the General Assembly in 2016 also warned: "Demonizing refugees or migrants offends profoundly against the values of dignity and equality for every human being, to which we have committed ourselves."

Exclusivism can easily lead to disconnection, discrimination and violation. "This goal of peace and security, however is not to be found merely in some ideal future society"[61].

It can happen now, in a modern island which gave birth to the Suffrage Movement, Anti-Fascist movements such as London Black Revolutionaries, the UK Occupy Movement, the UK LGBT Movement, and the Social Action and Research Foundation. We need education, communication, inspiration, courageous actions, and experiential learning: reaching out to cherish diversity while respecting the dignity of every human being. This connects also with the educational model of the UWC movement which states "Education

---

[61] Ikeda, VICTORY, p.15

requires active promotion of intercultural understanding and the development of genuine concern for others, founded on shared life experiences, and cooperative and collaborative living. This includes talking about and engaging with global issues in the pursuit of peace."

I am also personally committed to discuss the danger of passive tolerance with regards to the above matters: now is the time to value the beauty of a varied society, cherish differences which add value to the communities, and to dispel social tensions. Racism, discrimination and any form of intolerance are born out of fear.

I think it is my time to voice my vow to protect the sanctity of individuality.

> *Just as cherry, plum, peach and damson blossoms*
> *all possess their own unique qualities, each person is unique.*
> *We cannot become someone else.*
> *The important thing is that we live true to ourselves*
> *and cause the great flower of our lives to blossom.*
> [Daisaku Ikeda]

Change starts now.

It starts here.

It starts with me.

Unless we live fully,
not "sometime" in the future,
but right now,
true fulfilment in life will forever elude us.
Rather than put things off till the future,
we should find meaning
in doing what we think is most important
right now
— setting our hearts aflame and igniting our lives.
Otherwise, we will not be able to lead an inspired existence.
[Daisaku Ikeda]

appendix

I have decided to add here some material I found useful along my journey. You will find poems, writings, explanations.

A bit of everything.

My hope is for you to find *your* material along your way, and then to pass it on.

the invitation – oriah mountain dreamer[62]

It doesn't interest me what you do for a living.

I want to know what you ache for

and if you dare to dream of meeting your heart's longing.

It doesn't interest me how old you are.

I want to know if you will risk looking like a fool for love,

for your dream, for the adventure of being alive.

It doesn't interest me what planets are squaring your moon.

I want to know if you have touched

the centre of your own sorrow,

if you have been opened by life's betrayals

or have become shrivelled and closed

from fear of further pain.

I want to know if you can sit with pain,

mine or your own,

without moving to hide it,

or fade it, or fix it.

I want to know if you can be with joy,

---

[62] Every client I see receives a copy of this poem. This is also my invitation to you. You can find more about the author and her work here: http://www.oriahmountaindreamer.com/

mine or your own;

if you can dance with wildness

and let the ecstasy fill you

to the tips of your fingers and toes

without cautioning us to be careful, be realistic,

remember the limitations of being human.

It doesn't interest me if the story you are telling me is true.

I want to know if you can disappoint another

to be true to yourself.

If you can bear the accusation of betrayal

and not betray your own soul.

If you can be faithless and therefore trustworthy.

I want to know if you can see Beauty

even when it is not pretty every day.

And if you can source your own life from its presence.

I want to know if you can live with failure,

yours and mine,

and still stand at the edge of the lake

and shout to the silver of the full moon, 'Yes.'

It doesn't interest me to know where you live

or how much money you have.

I want to know if you can get up

after the night of grief and despair,

weary and bruised to the bone

and do what needs to be done to feed the children.

It doesn't interest me who you know

or how you came to be here.

I want to know if you will stand

in the centre of the fire

with me

and not shrink back.

It doesn't interest me where or what

or with whom you have studied.

I want to know what sustains you from the inside

when all else falls away.

I want to know if you can be alone with yourself

and if you truly like the company you keep

in the empty moments.

trust

Brené Brown is a research professor / story-teller at the University of Houston. She has spent the past sixteen years studying courage, vulnerability, shame, and empathy and is the author of various bestsellers, including *Daring Greatly*, which you can find here: https://amzn.to/2ricCWT

Her TED talks on *The Power of Vulnerability* and *Listening to Shame* are some of the most watched. You can find them both here:

1. https://youtu.be/iCvmsMzlF7o, and

2. https://youtu.be/iCvmsMzlF7o

Her talk on Trust on the Super Soul Session on OWN is also another must; here is the link: http://www.oprah.com/own-supersoulsessions/brene-brown-the-anatomy-of-trust-video

Through the acronym B.R.A.V.I.N.G she is revealing the anatomy of trust. Following, you can find some notes re. Trust: please, be inspired by them while watching the video. After, use them as a reminder of how vital Trust is.

I found the images online: they are a wonderful production by Isabella El-Hasan. You can find her works here: https://bellaelhasan.wordpress.com/about/

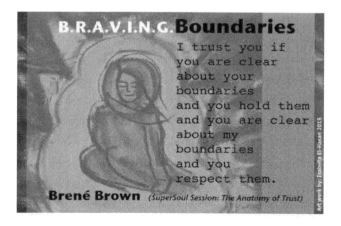

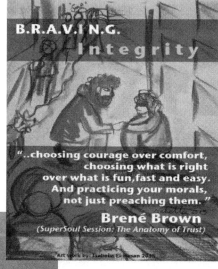

the crab bucket — elizabeth gilbert

Dear Ones -

A few months ago, I was on stage with my friend Rob Bell — minister, teacher, family man, great guy — and a woman in the audience asked him this question:

"I'm making all these important changes in my life, and I'm growing in so many new and exciting ways, but my family is resisting me. I feel like their resistance is holding me back. They seem threatened by my evolution as a person, and I don't know what to do about it."

Rob replied, "Well, of course they're threatened by your evolution as a person. You're disrupting their entire world order. Remember that a family is basically just a big crab bucket. Whenever one of the crabs tries to climb out and escape, the other crabs will grab hold of him, and try to pull him back down."

Which I thought was a VERY unexpected comment to come from a minister and a family man!

Rob surprised me even more, though, as he went on to say, "Families are institutions — just like a church, just like the army, just like a government. Their sense of their own stability depends upon keeping people in their correct place. Even if that stability is based on dysfunction or oppression, order must be maintained at all cost. When you try to move out of your 'correct place', you threaten everyone else's sense of order, and they may very likely try to pull you back down."

And sometimes, in our loyalty to family (or in our misplaced loyalty to the dysfunction that we are accustomed to) we might willingly

227

surrender and sacrifice our own growth, in order to not disrupt the family — and thus we stay in the crab bucket forever.

An example: Maybe you have started taking good care of your health recently — exercising and eating well — but your family undermines your efforts, either by making fun of you for your "weird" fitness routines, or by tempting you into overeating, in order to bring you back into your old behaviours.

Maybe you have quit drinking or smoking, and your family won't accept it, and they keep putting alcohol and cigarettes in front of you, as if it's no big deal.

Maybe you've embarked on a new spiritual path, and they find it so threatening that they mock you or shame you for it.

Maybe you've been working on pulling yourself out of depression, but they tell you that they liked you better the other way — that they preferred you when you were a shut-down and broken-down mess. (I've actually been told this by people I knew years ago: "I liked you better when you were depressed." Those words are such a blow to the soul. What are you even supposed to DO with that?)

Maybe you've come out of the closet, and your family members are all desperately trying to stuff you right back into that closet, so things will feel "normal" again.

Maybe you've been going back to school, or you're trying to save money to travel, or you've been talking about moving to a new city, and your family subtly or (or not so subtly!) makes you aware that they don't approve: "Oh, so you think you're better than us now, Miss Fancy-Pants?"

All of this is crab bucket behaviour of the highest order, and you can count on it to flare up around the holidays.

Friend groups can do this to each other, too. My friend Rayya was a heroin addict for many years, and she saw the same phenomenon at play with her friends in the drug world: One junkie would try to get clean, and the other junkies would instantly pull her back down into the world of addiction again.

I've seen it happen, too, when friends try to sabotage another friend's efforts to get out of debt, or to move into better relationships or situations in life. (The mentality being: "If I can't get out of this crab bucket, NOBODY is getting out of this crab bucket.")

When I first got published, I was working as a bartender, and when I shared my happy news with co-workers, one of the managers at the bar said, in real anger, "Don't you DARE go be successful on us. That was not the agreement." (And, silently, I was like: "The agreement? What agreement?") That person never forgave me, actually, for aspiring to climb out of that crab bucket — so I had to disentangle myself, and move on.

Not every family (or tribe-like grouping) is like this, of course. Some tribes encourage their members not just to climb, but to SOAR, and sometimes even to fly away. That is true grace — to want somebody to grow, even if it means that they might outgrow you.

But all too often, there are those in your tribe who will try with all their might to hold you back, or to pull you down into the crab bucket again and again.

If that is happening in your life, you must identify it and resist it.

Establish your own code of honour, belief, or behaviour — and stand quietly strong within that code.

Don't ever let anyone stop you from growing or changing.

Don't forget who you are. Not who you WERE — but who you are. Most importantly, don't forget who you aspire to become. That's the most vital thing. (My husband always says that the most important thing is not how you feel about your past or your present, but how you imagine your future. Keep your eyes on that future — that's where you need to be heading.)

As Rob Bell said beautifully: "If people love you, they want you to grow. If somebody doesn't want you to grow, then you can call their feelings about you by many names...but you cannot call it love."

If somebody doesn't want you to grow, you call their feelings about you "anger", or "resentment", or "insecurity", or "dominance" — but it damn sure ain't love. Nobody ever held anyone back because of love.

So here's the takeaway: If it's time for you to grow, you have to grow.

If it's time for you to change, you have to change.

If it's time for you to move, you have to move.

If it's time for you to finally crawl out of that crab bucket, start crawling.

Holding yourself back in order to make all the other people in the bucket happy will not serve you, and — ultimately — it will not serve them, either.

Be loving, be compassionate, be gracious, be forgiving. But by God, be whoever you need to be — not just over the holidays, but always.

(And needless to say, if you are the crab at the bottom of the bucket who is holding back another crab from escaping, it might be time to summon up all your love and all your courage and gently, generously, LET GO. It won't be easy, but it might be the most important thing you ever do. You might even liberate yourself in the process.)

ONWARD and all love,
LG

the 12 Celestine Insights[63]

The First Insight . . . A Critical Mass

A new spiritual awakening is occurring in human culture, an awakening brought about by a critical mass of individuals who experience their lives as a spiritual unfolding, a journey in which we are led forward by mysterious coincidences.

The Second Insight . . . The Longer Now

This awakening represents the creation of a new, more complete worldview, which replaces a five-hundred-year-old preoccupation with secular survival and comfort. While this technological preoccupation was an important step, our awakening to life's coincidences is opening us up to the real purpose of human life on this planet, and the real nature of our universe.

The Third Insight . . . A Matter Of Energy

We now experience that we live not in a material universe, but in a universe of dynamic energy. Everything extant is a field of sacred energy that we can sense and intuit. Moreover, we humans can project our energy by focusing our attention in the desired direction…where attention goes, energy flows…influencing other energy systems and increasing the pace of coincidences in our lives.

---

[63] Please see https://www.celestinevision.com/the-12-celestine-insights/

The Fourth Insight . . . The Struggle For Power

Too often humans cut themselves off from the greater source of this energy and then feel weak and insecure. To gain energy, we tend to manipulate or force others to give us attention and their energy. When we successfully dominate others in this way, we feel more powerful, but they are left weakened and often fight back. Competition for scarce, human energy is the cause of all conflict between people.

The Fifth Insight . . . The Message Of The Mystics

Insecurity and violence ends when we experience an inner connection with divine energy within, a connection described by mystics of all traditions. A sense of lightness and buoyancy, along with the constant sensation of love, are measures of this connection. If these measures are present, the connection is real. If not, it is only pretended.

The Sixth Insight . . . Clearing The Past

The more we stay connected, the more we are acutely aware of those times when we lose connection, usually when we are under stress. In these times, we can see our own particular way of stealing energy from others. Once our manipulations are brought to personal awareness, our connection becomes more constant and we can discover our own growth path in life, and our spiritual mission—the personal way we can contribute to the world.

The Seventh Insight . . . Engaging The Flow

Knowing our personal mission further enhances the flow of mysterious coincidences as we are guided toward our destinies. First we have a question; then dreams, daydreams, and intuitions lead us towards the answers, which usually are synchronistically provided by the wisdom of another human being.

The Eighth Insight . . . The Interpersonal Ethic

We can increase the frequency of guiding coincidences by uplifting every person that comes into our lives. Care must be taken not to lose our inner connection in romantic relationships. Uplifting others is especially effective in groups where each member can feel energy of all the others. With children, this is extremely important for their early security and growth. By seeing the beauty in every face, we lift others into their wisest self, and increase the chances of hearing a synchronistic message.

The Ninth Insight . . .the Emerging Culture

As we all evolve toward the best completion of our spiritual missions, the technological means of survival will be fully automated as humans focus instead on synchronistic growth. Such growth will move humans into higher energy states, ultimately transforming our bodies into spiritual form, and uniting this dimension of existence with the after-life dimension. Thus, ending the cycle of birth and death.

The Tenth Insight . . . Holding The Vision

The Tenth Insight is the realization that throughout history, human beings have been unconsciously struggling to implement this "lived" spirituality on Earth. Each of us comes here on assignment, and as we pull this understanding into consciousness, we can remember a fuller birth vision of what we wanted to accomplish with our lives. Furthermore, we can remember a common world vision of how we will all work together to create a new spiritual culture. We know that our challenge is to hold this vision with intention and prayer every day.

The Eleventh Insight . . . Extending Prayer Fields

The Eleventh Insight is the precise method through which we hold the vision. For centuries, religious scriptures, poems, and philosophies have pointed to a latent power of mind within all of us that mysteriously helps to affect what occurs in the future. It has been called faith power, positive thinking, and the power of prayer. We are now taking this power seriously enough to bring a fuller knowledge of it into public awareness. We are finding that this prayer power is a field of intention, which moves out from us and can be extended and strengthened, especially when we connect with others in a common vision. This is the power through which we hold the vision of a spiritual world and build the energy in ourselves, and in others, to make this vision a reality.

The Twelfth Insight . . .

Armed with Divine confidence, we begin to take the next step to self-knowledge. We experience times when a greater sense of Divine begins to dwell within us. This indwelling feels like a sense of God's presence. We still have our personal identity, but this status become subservient to a complete consciousness of love, patience, and openness to action. For this presence to remain or get more powerful, we must be totally transcendent of our "Control Dramas," or moments where we do not act on our intuition of other people's best interest.

on Fear – adapted from Elizabeth Gilbert

"Dearest Fear:

Creativity and I are about to go on a road trip together.

I understand you'll be joining us, because you always do. I acknowledge that you believe you have an important job to do in my life, and that you take your job seriously. Apparently, your job is to induce complete panic whenever I'm about to do anything interesting—and, may I say, you are superb at your job.

So by all means, keep doing your job, if you feel you must.

But I will also be doing my job on this road trip, which is to work hard and stay focused. And Creativity will be doing its job, which is to remain stimulating and inspiring.

There's plenty of room in this vehicle for all of us, so make yourself at home, but understand this: Creativity and I are the only ones who will be making any decisions along the way. I recognize and respect that you are part of this family, and so I will never exclude you from our activities, but still—your suggestions will never be followed.

You're allowed to have a seat, and you're allowed to have a voice, but you are not allowed to have a vote. You're not allowed to touch the road maps; you're not allowed to suggest detours; you're not allowed to fiddle with the temperature. Dude, you're not even allowed to touch the radio.

But above all else, my dear old familiar friend, you are absolutely forbidden to drive."

whole-hearted living – by brené brown

1. Cultivate Authenticity – Let go of what people think about you – when you feel vulnerable, don't shrink, don't puff up, stand on your own sacred ground!

2. Cultivate Self-Compassion – Let go of perfectionism – practice health-striving self-talk and aspire to be a good-enoughist!

3. Cultivate a Resilient Spirit – Let go of numbing and powerlessness – lean into joy and discomfort, even when you feel vulnerable (or should I say, because you feel vulnerable, this is the time to...)

4. Cultivate Gratitude and Joy – Let go of scarcity – when you feel vulnerable the most, acknowledge the feeling and list what you are grateful for.

5. Cultivate Intuition and Trusting Faith – Let go of the need for certainty – when you feel uncertain, get quiet, find a place to be still so that you can really hear what you are saying, what your inner voice is saying, what your gut feeling is saying!

6. Cultivate Creativity – Let go of comparison – join a community that shares your values and enrol in a creative class... or simply feel the fear of the university platform and go and do it anyway. Show up!

7. Cultivate Play and Rest – Let go of exhaustion as a status symbol and productivity as self-worth – when things are going really well in your family, what did it look like? When things did go really well for you, for YOU, what did it look like? What did it feel like? Make an 'ingredients for joy and meaning' list with all the answers. And stick it in this book ;) and for the exhaustion: drink your water!

8. Cultivate Calm and Stillness — Let go of anxiety as a lifestyle — identify the emotions that will most likely spark your reactivity. Are those similar to previous ones? Have you journaled about it already? Any quotes in here that might help?

9. Cultivate Meaningful Work — Let go of self-doubt and "supposed to" — write down all your 'supposed to' list and use 'inspiring, competitive and creative' as a filter to make your decision instead

10. Cultivate Laughter, Song, and Dance — Let go of being cool and "always in control" — make an 'authentic me' play-list with songs that make you feel the most like yourself! And I mean your lovely self!

the 12 steps

In the name of freedom of choice, these are the 12 steps as used by the Celebrate Recovery groups. The following versions are taken from:

- *A Purpose-Driven Recovery Resource: A Recovery Program based on eight principles from the Beatitudes*; four volumes, by John Baker and Rick Warren. If you are interested, there are local groups of Celebrate Recovery, besides the usual AA meetings. I have been fortunate enough to meet Pastor John Baker when he delivered our training course in the 12-step of Celebrate Recovery in Derby.

Please, feel free to see also the following:

- *The Zen of Recovery*, by Mel Ash
- *Mindfulness and the 12 Steps*, by Therese Jacobs-Stewart
- *12 Steps on the Buddha's Path* – Bill, Buddha, and We

the steps

1. We admitted we were powerless over our addictions and compulsive behaviours, that our lives had become unmanageable.

"I know that nothing good lives in me, that is my sinful nature. For I have the desire to do what is good, but I cannot carry it out." (Romans 7:18)

2. We came to believe that a power greater than ourselves could restore us to sanity.

"For it is God who works in you to will and to act accordingly to his good purpose" (Philippians 2:13)

3. We made a decision to turn our lives and our wills over to the care of God.

Therefore, I urge you, brothers, in view of God's mercy, to offer your bodies as living sacrifices, holy and pleasing to God – this is your spiritual act of worship." (Romans 12:1)

4. We made a searching and fearless inventory of ourselves.

"Let us examine our ways and test them, and let us return to the Lord." (Lamentations 3:40)

5. We admitted to God, to ourselves, and to another human being the exact nature of our wrongs.

Therefore confess your sins to each other and pray for each other so that you may be healed." (James 5:16)

6. We were entirely ready to have God remove all these defects of character.

"Humble yourselves before the Lord, and he will lift you up.! (James, 4:10)

7. We humbly asked Him to remove all our shortcomings.

"If we confess our sins, he is faithful and just and will forgive us our sins and purify us from all unrighteousness." (1 John 1:9)

8. We made a list of all persons we had harmed and became willing to make amends to them all.

"Do onto others as you would have them do to you". (Luke 6:31)

9. We made a direct amends to such people whenever possible, except when to do so would injure them or others.

"Therefore, if you are offering your gift at the altar and there remember that your brother has something against you, leave your gift there in front of the altar. First go and be reconciled to your brother; then come and offer your gift." (Matthew 5:23-24)

10. We continued to take personal inventory and when we were wrong, promptly admitted it.

"So, if you think you are standing firm, be careful that you don't fall". (1 Corinthians 10:12)

11. We sought through prayer and meditation to improve our conscious contact with God, praying only for knowledge of His will for us and power to carry that out.

"Let the word of Christ dwell in you richly". (Colossians 3:16)

12. Having had a spiritual experience as the result of these steps, we try to carry this message to others and to practice these principles in all our affairs.

"Brothers, if someone is caught in a sin, you who are spiritual should restore him gently. But watch yourself, or you also may be tempted." (Galatians 6:1)

a human revolution in 12 steps

I have often thought about re-writing the 12 steps, the rebel way. One evening my dear friend Kerry handed me a copy of a 12-step approach as per Nichiren Buddhism. She doesn't exactly remember how she came to have these and there is no official endorsement of them by the SGI. Still, I have taken them as a starting point to develop my own personal idea of a 12-step approach, my way.

> *Those who fall to the ground*
> *get back on their feet*
> *by using the ground to push themselves up.*
> [Daisaku Ikeda]

1. I acknowledge my state of emotional pain and hence the lower worlds as my own fundamental darkness. I also know that I can change my situation once I take full responsibility for managing my life;

2. I meditate, chant, pray and seek support for the realisation that my spiritual practice elevates my life condition;

3. I remind myself of my desire and determination to wholeheartedly change my life state and carry out my own human revolution;

4. I am determined to work on myself for my own self-development in order to become a fully functioning and independent being;

5. I admit to myself first and then to whoever I believe need to know, my own vulnerability, weaknesses, hurts, and short-comings;

6. I am determined to transform any self-destructing character mindsets through Faith, Study, and Action;

7. I am determined to transform my life and to cultivate hope and a deep appreciation for Life itself;

8. I acknowledge that I have harmed myself and others; hence, I develop a willingness to not repeat the same mistakes;

9. I am aware that I need to make changes in my life which might include making amends to people I have hurt in the past, except when doing so could cause further harm to self, them, and others; I continue to meditate, chant, and pray for their well-being and the happiness of all living beings;

10. I am determined to continually connect with my Buddha-nature and wisdom in order to be aware of any short-comings and to promptly change my behaviour;

11. With a constant seeking spirit, I sincerely pray, chant, and meditate in order to understand my Call and Mission, and to reveal my strength, courage, and determination to carry out same;

12. I am determined to awaken to my Buddha-nature by striving my courage and passion to transform my karma and support others on their path of discovery. I embrace the challenges of daily life as a mean to deepen my Faith, strengthen my resolve to live a joyful life, and actively seek to establish an everlasting status of Peace.

the Ten Worlds[64]

Buddhism identifies Ten Worlds--ten states or conditions of life that we experience within our lives, moving from one to another at any moment according to our interactions with our environment and those around us. Each of us possesses the potential to experience all ten, from the prison-like despair and self-hatred of Hell to the expansive joy and wisdom of Buddhahood.

The Ten Worlds are Hell, Hunger, Animality, Anger, Humanity, Heaven, Learning, Realization, Bodhisattva and Buddhahood. By strengthening our spiritual lives through the practice of chanting Nam-myoho-renge-kyo, Nichiren Buddhism teaches that rather than being at the mercy of our surroundings we can develop the ability to set our own direction and spend more of our lives in the more positive life states.

Each of us has a tendency to gravitate toward a particular life state, and if this is one of the lower worlds, great suffering can be caused to ourselves and those around us. Through raising up our life condition which manifests in the Ten Worlds, we can bring out the positive aspects of any situation we find ourselves in.

---

[64] As from http://www.sgi.org/resources/introductory-materials/ten-worlds.html. You will be able to find more info on the SGI pages and a downloadable pdf version of this description, too.

The world of Bodhisattva is a state of compassion in which we devote ourselves to the welfare and happiness of others. Buddhahood is a state of completeness and perfect freedom filled with wisdom, vitality, and courage in which even overcoming challenges becomes a source of joy.

Hell: A state of suffering and despair in which we perceive we have no freedom of action. It is characterized by the impulse to destroy ourselves and everything around us.

Hunger: The state of being controlled by an insatiable desire for money, power, status etc. While desires are inherent in any of the Ten Worlds, in this state we are at the mercy of our cravings and cannot control them.

Animality: In this state, we are ruled by instinct with neither reason nor moral sense nor the ability to make long-range judgments. We operate by the law of the jungle and will not hesitate to take advantage of those weaker than ourselves and fawn on those who are stronger.

Anger: Here, awareness of ego emerges, but it is a selfish, greedy, distorted ego, determined to best others at all costs and seeing everything as a potential threat to itself. In this state we value only ourselves and tend to hold others in contempt.

Humanity (also called Tranquillity): This is a flat, passive state of life, from which we can easily shift into the lower four worlds. While we may generally behave in a humane fashion in this state, we are highly vulnerable to strong external influences.

Heaven (or Rapture): This is a state of intense joy stemming, for example, from the fulfilment of some desire, a sense of physical well-being, or inner contentment. Though intense, the joy experienced in this state is short-lived and also vulnerable to external influences.

The six states from Hell to Heaven are called the six paths or six lower worlds. Any happiness or satisfaction to be gained in these states depends totally upon circumstances and is therefore transient and subject to change. In these six lower worlds, we base our entire happiness, indeed our whole identity, on externals.

The next two states, Learning and Realization, come about when we recognize that everything experienced in the six paths is impermanent, and we begin to seek some lasting truth. Unlike the six paths, which are passive reactions to the environment, these four higher states are achieved through deliberate effort.

Learning: In this state, we seek the truth through studying the teachings or experience of others.

Realization: In this state we seek the truth not through others' teachings but through our own direct perception of the world.

Having realized the impermanence of things, people in these states have won a measure of independence and are no longer a prisoner to their own reactions as in the six paths. However, they often tend to be contemptuous of people in the six paths who have not yet reached this understanding. In addition, their search for truth is primarily self-oriented, so there is a great potential for egotism in these two states.

Bodhisattva: Bodhisattvas are those who aspire to achieve enlightenment and at the same time are equally determined to enable all other beings to do the same. Conscious of the bonds that link us to all others, in this state we realize that any happiness we alone enjoy is incomplete, and we devote ourselves to alleviating others' suffering. Those in this state find their greatest satisfaction in altruistic behaviour.

Buddhahood: Buddhahood is a dynamic state that is difficult to describe. We can partially describe it as a state of perfect freedom, in which we are enlightened to the ultimate truth of life. It is characterized by infinite compassion and boundless wisdom. In this state, we can resolve harmoniously what appear from the standpoint of the nine worlds to be insoluble contradictions. A Buddhist sutra describes the attributes of the Buddha's life as a true self, perfect freedom from karmic bonds throughout eternity, a life purified of illusion, and absolute happiness.

journaling: a discipline against self-doubt

There is a myriad of benefits to journaling, and everyone should consider keeping a daily journal. However, one of the obstacles that people face when they want to pick up the practice of journaling is that they don't know what to write about.

So, here is a bit of extra inspiration:

1. What scares you?
2. Do you have a plan? Do you need a plan? Have you had a plan fall spectacularly to pieces?
3. Are you a worrier? Is there a particular worry that you can't shake? How do you cope with worry?
4. Nobody knows that I . . .
5. "Write a list of questions to which you urgently need answers."
6. The voices in my head say that. . .
7. Write the words you need to hear.
8. Dear _____, it weighs on me that I never told you . . .
9. The biggest lie I've ever told is . . .
10. Is there anything you feel guilty about? Is there anything you need to be forgiven for?
11. What's the worst thing you've ever done?
12. What's your secret desire?
13. What's the most outrageous thing you've ever done?
14. The most terrifying moment of my life was . . .
15. The most fun I've ever had . . .

16.The most surprised I've ever been . . .

17.The most disappointed I've ever been . . .

18.What are you looking forward to the most?

19.Three things you can't go without.

20.Three things you want in a relationship.

21.If you had to evacuate your home because of a natural disaster, what three things would you take with you?

22.The Holiday traditions I most look forward to . . .

23.Did you ever get lost?

24.Did you ever run away from home?

25.As a child, what did you want to be when you grew up?

26.What's your first memory?

27.What is your most vivid memory of the kitchen in your childhood?

28.What makes you unique?

29.How do you stand out from the crowd?

30.What are your best character traits?

31.What are you really good at?

32.How would you describe yourself?

33.What character traits do you need to work on?

34.What are some of your idiosyncrasies?

35.How do you think others see you when they meet you for the first time?

36.List 20 things that represent passion to you.

37.Write 100 things you want to do by the end of the (following) year.

38. How can you give back happiness to those who bring you joy?

39. How do you feel when you witness happiness?

40. Write a poem about the sound of happiness.

41. Where does happiness come from?

42. Who do you know that always shows happiness?

43. How can you bring happiness to…?

44. How can you encourage happiness?

45. What things make you happiest?

46. How can you begin recognizing happy moments each day?

47. Does happiness give you energy?

48. What can you accomplish when you're happy?

49. What does it mean to find the silver lining in a situation?

50. How do you show your happiness?

51. What happens when you feel happy?

52. Write about the way smiles look.

53. How do you feel when someone rains on your parade?

54. How can you bring your neighbours happiness?

55. What things or people make you smile?

56. Why is it so important to promote the sharing of happiness?

57. How do you celebrate happiness in your life?

58. Do you ever smile even when you don't feel like it?

59. How do you think others feel when you rain on their parades?

60. How do you feel when others are happy?

61. What makes you feel enthusiastic?

62. How do you feel when you express your happiness?

63. What would the world be like if there were more happiness?

64.Write a letter of thanks to someone who makes you happy.

65.Write a story about a world where no sadness existed.

66.Do you think happiness can make people healthier?

67.How can happiness be contagious?

68.How can I make this journey of mine, last?

69.Why am I not journalling?

70.What words are you expecting to hear?

"Do not believe in anything
simply because you have heard it.
Do not believe in anything
because it is spoken and rumoured by many.
Do not believe in anything
simply because it is found written in your religious books.
Do not believe in anything
merely on the authority of your teachers and elders.
Do not believe in traditions
because they have been handed down for many generations.
But after observation and analysis,
when you find that anything agrees with reason
and is conducive to the good and benefit of one and all,
then accept it and live up to it."

[Dzogchen Ponlop Rinpoche - Rebel Buddha]

references & bibliography

Ackerman, R.J. (2002) *Perfect Daughters: Adult Daughters of Alcoholics*. Health Communications

Ackerman, R.J., (1195) *Before it's too late*, Deerfield Beach, Health Communications

Argyle, M. (1973). *The Psychology of Interpersonal Behaviour*. Harmondsworth. Penguin Books Ltd.

Ash, M., (1993). *The Zen of Recovery*, New York, Penguin Putnam

Baker, J. (1991). *Celebrate Recovery Participants' Guide 1-4*, Zondervan

Beattie, M., (1990) *The Language of Letting Go*, Centre City, Hazelden

Beattie, M., (1992) *Codependent No More*, Centre City, Hazelden

Beattie, M., (2011) *Codependent No More, Workbook*, Centre City, Hazelden

Bridges, W. *Transitions – Making Sense of Life's Changes*, Da Capo Press, 2004

Burnett, D., *The Idiot Brain*, London, Guardian Books, 2016

Causton, R. (1995). *The Buddha in Daily Life. An Introduction to the Buddhism of Nichiren Daishonin*. London, Random House.

Cooper, M. (2015). *Existential Psychotherapy and Counselling*. London, SAGE.

Cori, J.L., (2010) *The Emotionally Absent Mother*, New York, The Experiment

de Botton, A., (2012) *Religion for Atheists*, London, Penguin Books

Dickson, A. (1982) *A Woman in your own right. Assertiveness and You*. London, TJ International Ltd

Dryden, W. (1992). *Integrative and Eclectic Therapy. A Handbook*. Buckingham, Open Univ. Pr.

Eagleman, D., (2015) *The Brain*, Edinburgh, Canongate Books

Egan, G. (2010). *The Skilled Helper*. Belmont Brooks Cole, Cengage Learning.

Eldredge, John and Stasi (2005) *Captivating. Unveiling the Mystery of a Woman's Soul*. Nashville. Thomas Nelson, Inc.

Epstein, M., (2013) *Thoughts without a Thinker*, New York, Basic Books

Erikson, J.M., (1982) *The Life Cycle Completed*, Rikan Enterprise

Frankl, V. (2011). *Man's Search for Ultimate Meaning*. London, Rider.

Geringer Woititz, Janet (1983) *Adult Children of Alcoholics*. Deerfield Beach. USA

Greenberger, D. and Padesky, C.A. (1995). *Mind over Mood. Change how you feel by changing the way you think*. London. The Guilford Press.

Griffith, J. and Griffith, M. (2003). *Encountering the Sacred in Psychotherapy*. New York Guilford Press.

Gross, R.D. (1991). *Psychology. The Science of Mind and Behaviour*. Sevenoaks. Hodder and Stoughton Ltd.

Grozs, S. (2013). *The Examined Life*. London. Chatto & Windus

Hanson, R., (2009) *Buddha's Brain*, Oakland, Raincoast Books

Henderson, H. and Ikeda, D. (2004) *Planetary Citizenship. Your Values, Beliefs and Actions can shape a Sustainable World*. Middleway Press

Hough, M. (1994). *A Practical Approach to Counselling*. Harlow, Longman Group Ltd.

Ikeda, D. (2001) *For the Sake of PEACE. Seven Paths to Global Harmony*, Middleway Press

Ikeda, D. (2010) Discussions on YOUTH, World Tribune Press

Ikeda, D. (2013) *The Teachings for VICTORY*, Vol 1-3, World Tribune Press

Ikeda, D. (2015) *The Wisdom for creating Happiness and Peace, Vol. 1 HAPPINESS*, Eternal Ganges Press

Ikeda, D. (2015) *The Wisdom for creating Happiness and Peace, Vol. 2.1 HUMAN REVOLUTION*, Eternal Ganges Press

Ikeda, D. *et. al.* (2010) *The WISDOM of the Lotus Sutra*, Vol. 1-6, World Tribune Press

Jacobs, M. (2010). *Psychodynamic Counselling in Action*. London. Sage Publications Ltd.

Jacobs-Stewart, T. (2010). *Mindfulness and the 12 Steps*, Center City, Hazelden

Johnson, R.A., (1991) *Owning you own Shadow*, New York, HarperCollins

Klein, M. and Riviere, J., (1964) *Love, Hate and Reparation*, Norton Library

Lee Cori, Jasmin (2010) *The Emotionally Absent Mother*. New York. The Experiment, LLC

Ley, J., (2013) *Freudian Slips*, London, Michael O'Mara Books

Lickerman, A. (2012). *The Undefeated Mind*. Deerfield Beach, Health Communications Inc.

Lipton, B.H., (2005) *The Biology of Belief*, London, Hay House

Mearns, D. et al. (2008). *Person-Centred Counselling in Action*. London. Sage Publications Ltd.

Osho (2009) *The book of Wisdom. The Heart of Tibetan Buddhism*, Osho Media International

Parkin, John (2012) *f**t therapy. The profane way to profound happiness*. London. Hay House

Ponlop, D. Rinpoche (2011). *Rebel Buddha: A Guide to a Revolution of Mind*, Shambhala Publications Inc

Potter, C., (2014) *How to make a Human Being*, London, Harper Collins

Reeves, G. (2008) *The Lotus Sutra. A contemporary translation of a Buddhist Classic*, Boston, Wisdom Publication

Rowan, J. (1998). *The Reality Game*, 2nd edition. London, Routledge.

S., Laura (2006). *12 Steps on Buddha's Path*, Somerville, Wisdom Publications Inc.

Sanders, P. (2011). *First Steps in Counselling. A Students' Companion for Introductory Courses*. Ross on Wye. PCCS Books.

Scott Peck, M. (2012). *The Road less travelled*. London. The Random House.

Slater, A. and Bremner G., (2003) *An Introduction to Developmental Psychology*, Oxford, Blackwell Publishing

Spinelli, E., (2005) *The Interpreted World*, London, SAGE

Tolan, J. (2012). *Skills in Person-Centred Counselling and Psychotherapy*. London. Sage Publications Ltd.

Trower, P. et al. (2011). *Cognitive Behavioural Counselling in Action*. Sage Publications Ltd.

van der Kolk, B., (2014) *The Body keeps the Score*, Penguin Books

van Deurzen, E. (2015). *Paradox and Passion in Psychotherapy: An Existential Approach*, 2nd Edition. Chichester, John Wiley & Sons.

van Deurzen, E., (2009) *Psychotherapy and the Quest for Happiness*, London, SAGE

WND (1999) *The Writings of Nichiren Daishonin*, vol. 1 and vol. 2, Soka Gakkai

Woodman, M. (1985) *The Pregnant Virgin. A Process of Psychological Transformation*. Toronto. Inner City Books

Woolfe, R. and Palmer, S. (2000). *Integrative and Eclectic Counselling and Psychotherapy*. London, SAGE

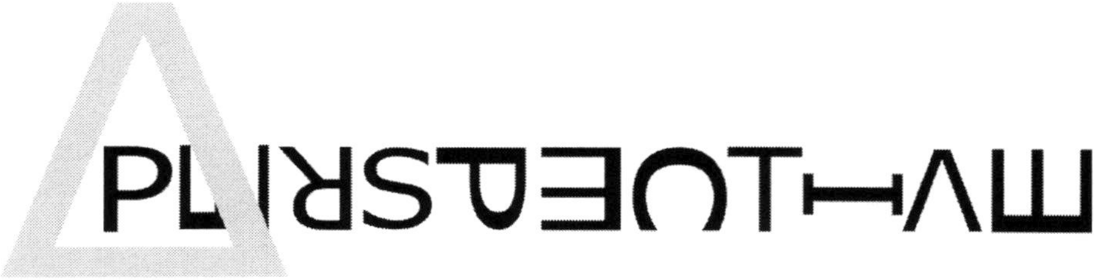

Printed in Great Britain
by Amazon